Revitalizing Prosperity

Revitalizing Prosperity

NAVIGATING THE GLOBAL ECONOMIC RECOVERY POST-PANDEMIC

Rayan Musk

Mohammed Altaf Hussain

Contents

Table of Content

Introduction

1. Brief overview of the unprecedented challenges posed by the COVID-19 pandemic
2. Importance of global economic recovery for sustainable development
3. Outline of key themes to be explored in subsequent chapters

Chapter 1 The Pandemic's Impact on Global Economies
1.1 Analysis of the immediate economic fallout during the pandemic
1.2 Examination of sectors most affected and the disparities in impact
1.3 Lessons learned from the crisis and the need for adaptive economic strategies

Chapter 2 Policy Responses and Stimulus Measures
2.1 Assessment of government interventions and fiscal policies worldwide
2.2 Successful policy implementations
2.3 Critique of potential shortcomings and long-term implications

Chapter 3 The Role of International Cooperation
3.1 Exploration of collaborative efforts among nations and global institutions
3.2 Examination of global initiatives aimed at economic recovery
3.3 Challenges and opportunities in fostering international solidarity

Chapter 4 Innovations in Technology and Digital Transformation
4.1 Impact of technological advancements on economic recovery
4.2 Industries leveraging digital transformation
4.3 Prospects for sustained growth through technological innovation

Chapter 5 Sustainable Development and Green Initiatives
5.1 Importance of incorporating sustainability into economic recovery plans

Introduction

Directly following the exceptional worldwide difficulties presented by the Coronavirus pandemic, the world winds up at a crucial point ever. As countries wrestle with the multi-layered effects of the emergency, there exists an aggregate basic to graph a course towards a revived thriving. The excursion toward monetary recuperation is perplexing and interconnected, requiring a nuanced comprehension of the worldwide scene, inventive methodologies, and cooperative endeavors across borders.

The pandemic, a seismic occasion that rose above topographical limits, has made a permanent imprint on social orders and economies around the world. It uncovered weaknesses in medical services frameworks, disturbed worldwide stockpile chains, and exposed the advanced gap. States were constrained to carry out phenomenal measures, for example, lockdowns and financial boost bundles to relieve the quick effect, however the repercussions keep on resounding.

As we stand on the cusp of another time, it is fundamental to perceive that financial recuperation isn't simply a re-visitation of pre-pandemic standards. All things considered, it requests a change in outlook, a recalibration of needs, and a guarantee to building a stronger and comprehensive worldwide economy. This requires a takeoff from conventional models of development and improvement, embracing advancement, maintainability, and social value as core values.

One of the essential difficulties in exploring the post-pandemic financial scene is the distinct disparity in recuperation directions among countries. While certain nations display powerful bounce back, others wrestle with delayed financial slumps, fueling existing imbalances. Tending to this difference requires a planned worldwide exertion, incorporating strategy coordination, monetary help, and innovation move to enable countries with less assets.

Moreover, the job of innovation in forming the financial recuperation couldn't possibly be more significant. The pandemic sped up computerized change, making it a key part for strength and development.

The Fourth Modern Unrest is as of now not a far off prospect however a quick reality that requests proactive strategies to outfit the capability of man-made reasoning, robotization, and other extraordinary innovations. As countries competition to digitize their economies, finding some kind of harmony among development and the likely relocation of occupations is a basic test that should be explored with foreknowledge.

Supportability arises as a crucial support point in the mission for revived flourishing. The pandemic highlighted the association between human prosperity and the soundness of the planet. As countries modify, there is a phenomenal chance to install ecological manageability into monetary recuperation plans. Interests in environmentally friendly power, green framework, and round economies might drive monetary development at any point as well as moderate the dangers presented by environmental change.

Inclusivity should be at the core of the monetary recuperation plan. The pandemic lopsidedly impacted weak populaces, fueling imbalances in medical services, training, and work. To construct an additional fair future, legislatures and organizations should embrace strategies that advance social consideration, address variations, and guarantee that the advantages of monetary recuperation arrive at all portions of society. This incorporates reconsidering schooling and preparing projects to outfit people with the abilities required in the advancing position market.

Worldwide exchange, a foundation of financial interconnectedness, requires a recharged concentration to impel the world towards thriving. The pandemic uncovered the delicacy of worldwide inventory chains, inciting a reassessment of the customary exchange worldview. Nations are reconsidering their conditions and investigating provincial organizations to upgrade flexibility. A promise to open and fair exchange rehearses, combined with the evacuation of boundaries, will be pivotal in encouraging a favorable climate for worldwide monetary recuperation.

The monetary scene, as well, assumes a urgent part in the post-pandemic recuperation. National banks and monetary organizations have conveyed remarkable money related measures to balance out economies during the emergency. As countries progress from emergency reaction to recuperation, the test lies in loosening up these actions without setting off unfriendly results. Finding some kind of harmony between keeping up with monetary steadiness and forestalling expansion or monetary unsteadiness requires cautious adjustment and global collaboration.

1. **Brief overview of the unprecedented challenges posed by the COVID-19 pandemic**
   The coming of the Coronavirus pandemic denoted a turning point in present day history, pushing the world into a cauldron of remarkable difficulties. As the novel Covid, SARS-CoV-2, spread across landmasses, it fashioned destruction on worldwide wellbeing, economies, and cultural standards. The greatness of the emergency was faltering, uncovering weaknesses in medical services frameworks, upsetting laid out methods of administration, and revealing the delicacy of interconnected worldwide stockpile chains.

At the front of the pandemic's effect was the cost for human wellbeing. The fast and harmful nature of the infection prompted a mind-boggling burden on medical services frameworks around the world. Emergency clinics wrestled with deficiencies of basic clinical supplies, ventilators, and staff, as the sheer volume of Coronavirus cases stressed their abilities to the verge. The cost for medical services laborers, the cutting edge legends fighting the infection, was tremendous, both genuinely and inwardly.

The pandemic likewise disentangled the cultural texture, revealing firmly established disparities. Weak populaces, including the old and those with prior medical issue, confronted unbalanced chances. Differences in admittance to medical care and financial assets turned out to be extremely obvious, enhancing existing separation points inside social orders. The conclusion of schools and interruptions to normal financial exercises lopsidedly impacted low-pay networks, fueling instructive and monetary disparities.

Economies overall were not safe to the seismic shockwaves of the pandemic. The burden of lockdowns and limitations on development, carried out to check the spread of the infection, set off an uncommon financial slump. Organizations covered, supply chains broke, and millions regarded themselves as jobless or underemployed. The worldwide economy contracted at a disturbing rate, diving into a downturn that repeated the monetary disturbances of the previous 100 years.

States confronted an unenviable test in endeavoring to offset general wellbeing goals with the monetary aftermath. Enormous financial boost bundles were carried on a mission to help organizations, safeguard occupations, and give a wellbeing net to people. Nonetheless, the sheer size of the emergency extended the monetary limits of even the most strong economies, prompting expanding public obligations and financial vulnerabilities.

The pandemic's troublesome effect reached out to the domain of instruction. With schools and colleges shutting their actual ways to control the infection's spread, the training area wrestled with an extraordinary shift to remote learning. This change, while fundamental for keeping up with instructive progression, exacerbated existing variations in admittance to innovation and quality schooling. Understudies and teachers confronted the difficulties of adjusting to virtual homerooms, featuring the requirement for imaginative arrangements and computerized foundation.

The social and mental cost of the pandemic was similarly significant. Lockdowns and social removing estimates upset shared exercises, restricting human cooperation and stressing psychological wellness. The vulnerability encompassing the span and seriousness of the emergency powered tension and stress, making a worldwide emotional wellness challenge. The deficiency of lives, intensified by the powerlessness to grieve and lament aggregately, added one more layer of intricacy to the human experience during the pandemic.

In addition, the emergency uncovered the weaknesses and restrictions of world-wide administration structures. The absence of a planned worldwide reaction in the beginning phases of the pandemic highlighted the deficiencies of existing systems for tending to worldwide wellbeing crises. Nationalistic inclinations and international strains additionally confounded endeavors to team up on a brought together front against a shared adversary, blocking the opportune trade of data, assets, and mastery.

As the world wrestled with the prompt effects of the pandemic, it likewise stood up to the drawn out suggestions and the requirement for an essential vision to explore the post-Coronavirus scene. The pandemic filled in as an impetus for sped up development and variation. Mainstream researchers overall teamed up at a remarkable speed to create and circulate immunizations, displaying the potential for aggregate activity notwithstanding worldwide difficulties.

2. **Importance of global economic recovery for sustainable development**

The significance of worldwide monetary recuperation in the post-Coronavirus time couldn't possibly be more significant, as it frames the key part for accomplishing supportable improvement on an overall scale. The pandemic's sweeping effects have exposed the interconnectedness of economies, social orders, and the climate, highlighting the criticalness of cultivating recuperation procedures that are vigorous as well as practical and comprehensive.

At the core of the talk on worldwide monetary recuperation is the idea of supportability. Feasible turn of events, as expressed by the Unified Countries, is a comprehensive methodology that tries to address the issues of the present without compromising the capacity of people in the future to address their own issues.

The Coronavirus emergency has emphasizd the basic of integrating supportability into monetary recuperation endeavors, perceiving the multifaceted linkages between financial prosperity, social value, and ecological wellbeing.

Financial recuperation, when sought after with supportability as a core value, turns into an impetus for tending to squeezing natural difficulties. The pandemic-actuated stoppage prompted impermanent decreases in fossil fuel by-products and further developed air quality in certain locales. Nonetheless, these increases are transient, and a feasible recuperation should focus on decoupling monetary development from natural corruption. Putting resources into clean energy, advancing round economies, and consolidating eco-accommodating advancements into creation processes are essential strides toward alleviating the biological effect of monetary exercises.

Besides, a maintainable financial recuperation lines up with the worldwide obligation to accomplishing the Unified Countries Reasonable Improvement Objectives (SDGs). These 17 interconnected objectives envelop many targets, including neediness annihilation, zero yearning, great wellbeing and prosperity, quality schooling, orientation correspondence, clean water and disinfection, reasonable and clean energy, respectable work and monetary development, industry, advancement and foundation, diminished disparities, maintainable urban areas and networks, capable utilization and creation, environment activity, life beneath water, life ashore, harmony, equity, and solid organizations, and associations for the objectives.

The exchange between monetary recuperation and the SDGs is clear in the acknowledgment that financial development, when comprehensive and manageable, fills in as a way to accomplish a considerable lot of these goals. For example, fair work and monetary development (SDG 8) are results of a recuperating economy as well as necessary parts that add to destitution decrease (SDG 1) and diminished imbalances (SDG 10). Additionally, practical creation and utilization (SDG 12) are fundamental for limiting ecological effects, tending to environmental change (SDG 13), and guaranteeing the dependable utilization of assets.

Inclusivity is an essential component chasing manageable monetary recuperation. The Coronavirus pandemic exacerbated existing social and monetary disparities, lopsidedly influencing weak populaces. Ladies, minorities, and low-pay networks confronted increased difficulties, from employment misfortunes and instructive disturbances to restricted admittance to medical services. A practical recuperation should focus on strategies and drives that span these holes, guaranteeing that the advantages of financial development are fairly conveyed.

One vital part of comprehensive recuperation is the accentuation on instruction and ability improvement. The pandemic upset customary schooling systems, revealing abberations in admittance to remote learning.

A practical recuperation requires designated endeavors to address these inconsistencies, utilizing innovation to give equivalent instructive open doors. By putting resources into schooling, countries can engage their populaces with the abilities expected to partake in the developing position market, cultivating financial strength and diminishing disparity.

Moreover, the idea of inclusivity stretches out to the worldwide stage. Global participation is essential for a maintainable monetary recuperation, as no country exists in detachment. The pandemic unmistakably represented the weaknesses intrinsic in a divided worldwide reaction. To construct a stronger and interconnected world, countries should team up on numerous fronts, including immunization dispersion, exchange, innovation move, and monetary help to less created districts.

Exchange, a foundation of the worldwide economy, assumes a significant part in the recuperation cycle. Open and fair exchange rehearses add to monetary development, work creation, and neediness decrease. Nonetheless, the pandemic uncovered weaknesses in worldwide stockpile chains, provoking a reconsideration of exchange elements. A reasonable recuperation involves changes that upgrade the flexibility of supply chains, focus on fair exchange rehearses, and guarantee that monetary advantages are shared across countries.

The monetary area, as well, is indispensable to the supportability of financial recuperation. The pandemic incited exceptional money related measures to settle economies, however loosening up these actions without setting off unfavorable outcomes represents a huge test. Facilitated endeavors among national banks and global monetary establishments are fundamental to explore the sensitive harmony between keeping up with financial solidness and forestalling expansion or monetary insecurity.

Notwithstanding inclusivity and ecological contemplations, innovation arises as a vital driver of practical financial recuperation. The Fourth Modern Upset, described by headways in man-made reasoning, mechanization, and advanced advancements, is reshaping ventures and work markets. A practical recuperation embraces the extraordinary capability of innovation while tending to worries about work relocation and the computerized partition.

Bridling the force of innovation for maintainable improvement includes key interests in computerized foundation, network protection, and the advancement of computerized abilities. By cultivating development and utilizing innovation for social and financial strengthening, countries can situate themselves at the very front of the advanced economy. Besides, innovation assumes a critical part in tending to worldwide difficulties, from further developing medical care conveyance and training admittance to improving ecological observing and reaction capacities.

3. **Outline of key themes to be explored in subsequent chapters**

In the resulting parts, a far reaching investigation of key subjects connected with worldwide financial recuperation and supportable improvement will unfurl. The overall goal is to dive into the complicated exchange between monetary, social, and ecological aspects, offering a nuanced comprehension of the difficulties and valuable open doors that characterize the post-Coronavirus scene.

The main topical string rotates around the natural basic implanted chasing feasible monetary recuperation. The sections will dive into the significant effect of the pandemic-actuated stoppage on fossil fuel byproducts and air quality, perceiving the transient idea of these increases. The accentuation will move towards explaining the methodologies expected to decouple financial development from natural debasement. Interest in clean energy, the advancement of round economies, and the mix of eco-accommodating advancements into creation cycles will be analyzed as vital parts of a maintainable recuperation.

The subsequent key subject habitats on the Assembled Countries Practical Advancement Objectives (SDGs) and their inherent association with monetary recuperation. An exhaustive examination will unwind the interlinkages between financial development, social value, and ecological supportability as exemplified in the SDGs.

The investigation will reach out to explicit objectives like respectable work and financial development, neediness annihilation, diminished imbalances, and economical creation and utilization. Understanding how financial recuperation can act as an impetus for accomplishing these worldwide targets will be a point of convergence.

Inclusivity arises as a third focal topic, recognizing the basic of guaranteeing that the advantages of monetary recuperation are evenhandedly circulated across different cultural layers. The sections will dig into the exacerbated social and monetary imbalances exposed by the pandemic, with a specific spotlight on weak populaces like ladies, minorities, and low-pay networks. Instructive differences and the job of innovation in spanning these holes will be investigated as fundamental parts of comprehensive recuperation.

A fourth subject includes the worldwide element of recuperation, stressing the vitality of global participation. The pandemic featured the weaknesses innate in a divided worldwide reaction, highlighting the requirement for cooperative endeavors on different fronts. Exchange elements, innovation move, immunization dissemination, and monetary help to less created locales will be inspected as basic parts of an internationally interconnected recuperation system.

Exchange, comprising a foundation of the worldwide economy, shapes an unmistakable fifth topic. The parts will examine the job of open and fair exchange works on cultivating monetary development, work creation, and destitution decrease. Notwithstanding, the pandemic-incited interruptions to worldwide inventory chains require a reconsideration of exchange elements. Changes pointed toward improving the flexibility of supply chains and guaranteeing evenhanded monetary advantages across countries will be investigated inside and out.

The 6th subject communities on the monetary area's part in the manageability of financial recuperation. Phenomenal money related measures were sent to balance out economies during the pandemic, however the loosening up of these actions represents a critical test. The sections will enlighten the sensitive equilibrium expected to keep up with monetary dependability without setting off antagonistic results like expansion or monetary flimsiness. Facilitated endeavors among national banks and global monetary establishments will be featured as critical to exploring this perplexing landscape.

Innovation as a groundbreaking power arises as a seventh topical string. The Fourth Modern Transformation, described by progressions in man-made reasoning, computerization, and advanced innovations, reshapes businesses and work markets. The parts will examine the extraordinary capability of innovation for reasonable turn of events, underscoring vital interests in advanced framework, network safety, and the improvement of computerized abilities. Addressing concerns connected with work removal and the computerized gap will be fundamental to understanding the positive effect of innovation on monetary recuperation.

Chapter 1

The Pandemic's Impact on Global Economies

The Coronavirus pandemic has made a permanent imprint on worldwide economies, setting off a seismic change on the planet's financial scene. The complex effect of the pandemic reaches out a long ways past the prompt wellbeing emergency, pervading each feature of society and testing the flexibility of countries. As we dig into the significant repercussions, it becomes clear that the pandemic isn't simply a wellbeing crisis; a financial pot has tried the underpinnings of monetary frameworks, supply chains, and strategy structures.

The most prompt and unmistakable impact of the pandemic on worldwide economies has been the serious constriction of monetary action. The inconvenience of lockdowns, travel limitations, and social separating estimates carried conventional monetary exercises to a crushing stop. Businesses like cordiality, the travel industry, and flight were especially hard-hit as lines shut, and buyers withdrew into a condition of mindfulness, modifying spending examples and needs. The unexpected and sharp decrease popular prompted a fountain of results, with organizations confronting terminations, mass cutbacks, and monetary misery.

The worldwide downturn set off by the pandemic is uncommon in its scale and fast beginning. Economies that were once flourishing ended up wrestling with negative development rates, rising joblessness, and monetary insecurity. The World Bank extended a 5.2% constriction in worldwide Gross domestic product in 2020, making it the most profound downturn since WWII. The financial aftermath has been unavoidable to the point that even countries with vigorous monetary limits attempted to send measures sufficiently significant to neutralize the slump.

The work market endured the worst part of the financial aftermath, with a great many specialists confronting employment misfortunes, vacations, or diminished working hours. The Worldwide Work Association (ILO) assessed that what could be compared to 255 million regular positions were lost in 2020, fueling existing disparities and compromising vocations universally. Weak gatherings, remembering casual specialists and those for problematic business, confronted uplifted gambles, extending social incongruities.

Little and medium-sized undertakings (SMEs), frequently hailed as the foundation of numerous economies, confronted intense difficulties during the pandemic. Many had to screen tasks, incapable to climate the monetary tempest. The disturbances in supply chains, combined with diminished purchaser spending, made a cascading type of influence that resonated through the whole business biological system. Legislatures all over the planet executed financial improvement bundles to help organizations, yet the sheer size of the monetary constriction extended the viability of these actions.

Worldwide exchange, a key part of monetary reliance, experienced critical disturbances as countries shut borders and focused on homegrown worries. Supply chains, finely tuned for effectiveness, uncovered their weakness as disturbances in a single district flowed across the globe. The pandemic exposed the dangers related with over-dependence on specific districts for basic parts, inciting a reassessment of worldwide inventory network systems. Protectionist feelings and exchange strains additionally confounded the worldwide exchange scene, raising worries about a retreat from globalization.

The monetary area, normally a balancing out force in financial emergencies, confronted its own arrangement of difficulties during the pandemic. National banks overall carried out uncommon financial measures to forestall a total monetary implosion. Loan costs were sliced, and monstrous liquidity infusions were conveyed to settle monetary business sectors. Be that as it may, the drawn out results of such measures, including the potential for expansion, resource bubbles, and monetary awkward nature, remain subjects of concern and discussion.

The pandemic-actuated monetary slump likewise highlighted the deficiencies of existing social wellbeing nets. The weakness of gig laborers, casual workers, and those in shaky business turned out to be extremely obvious as many wound up without admittance to joblessness benefits or different types of social help. The emergency revealed the requirement for complete social insurance frameworks that can endure the shockwaves of unanticipated emergencies and give a wellbeing net to all residents.

States confronted the overwhelming test of finding some kind of harmony between safeguarding general wellbeing and alleviating financial aftermath. The strategy reactions fluctuated broadly, mirroring the extraordinary conditions and limits of individual countries. A few executed severe lockdowns to control the infection's spread, forfeiting monetary movement for general wellbeing. Others embraced more permissive measures, meaning to offset wellbeing worries with the basic of keeping economies above water. The viability of these differed approaches stays a subject of progressing investigation, with illustrations to be learned for future emergencies.

The pandemic likewise uncovered the restrictions of worldwide administration structures in answering an emergency of such size. The absence of a planned worldwide reaction, especially in the beginning phases of the pandemic, featured the difficulties of preparing aggregate activity despite a worldwide danger. Nationalistic propensities and international pressures additionally convoluted endeavors to team up on a brought together front, impeding the ideal trade of data, assets, and skill.

The innovative scene saw the two difficulties and potential open doors during the pandemic. On one hand, the emergency sped up advanced change as remote work, web based business, and computerized correspondence became fundamental parts of day to day existence. Then again, the advanced separation turned out to be more articulated as differences in web access and computerized abilities thwarted the capacity of specific populaces to adjust to the new ordinary. The pandemic highlighted the basic of addressing these variations to guarantee evenhanded cooperation in the computerized economy.

As countries wrestle with the continuous difficulties of the pandemic, the center is moving towards financial recuperation and modifying. The progressive rollout of immunizations offers a hint of something better over the horizon, however the way to recuperation stays full of vulnerabilities. States are figuring out recuperation designs that go past transient improvement measures, stressing the requirement for flexibility, manageability, and inclusivity in revamping economies.

Manageability arises as a critical thought in the post-pandemic financial recuperation. The emergency exposed the interconnectedness of human prosperity and the strength of the planet.

As countries reconstruct, there is a developing acknowledgment that monetary recuperation should be lined up with natural manageability. Interests in environmentally friendly power, green foundation, and manageable practices are viewed as necessary parts of a strong and ecologically dependable recuperation.

Inclusivity is one more core value in forming the recuperation cycle. The abberations uncovered by the pandemic, whether regarding admittance to medical services, instructive open doors, or monetary assets, request designated endeavors to connect the holes. Comprehensive recuperation includes arrangements that focus on weak populaces, address social imbalances, and guarantee that the advantages of recuperation are shared impartially.

Innovation, playing had a urgent impact during the emergency, stays a focal topic in the recuperation story. The computerized change, when seen as a pattern, is presently a basic for organizations and social orders. Legislatures are zeroing in on computerized foundation, abilities advancement, and administrative structures to saddle the capability of innovation for financial recuperation. Adjusting the advantages of development with the expected dangers, like work dislodging, stays a basic test.

Worldwide participation is imperative in exploring the intricacies of worldwide monetary recuperation. The pandemic featured the requirement for cooperative endeavors on different fronts, from antibody appropriation and general wellbeing measures to exchange and monetary dependability. Building a stronger and interconnected world expects countries to rise above limited public interests and work all in all to address shared difficulties.

1.1 Analysis of the immediate economic fallout during the pandemic

The quick financial aftermath during the beginning phases of the Coronavirus pandemic was uncommon in its scale and speed, as countries wrestled with the double test of containing the infection's spread and moderating the serious disturbances to monetary exercises. The interconnectedness of the worldwide economy turned out to be extremely evident as the shockwaves resounded across businesses, supply chains, and monetary business sectors. This examination digs into the complex elements of the quick monetary aftermath, analyzing the disturbances in exchange, work markets, enterprises, and the monetary area.

One of the earliest and most discernible effects of the pandemic was the unexpected disturbance to worldwide stockpile chains. As the infection spread, nations carried out lockdowns and travel limitations, upsetting the creation and transportation of merchandise. The dependence on "in the nick of time" stock frameworks, pointed toward limiting costs through effective stockpile chains, ended up being a situation with two sides.

While these frameworks were successful in ordinary conditions, the pandemic presented their weakness to shocks. Ventures confronted deficiencies of basic parts, prompting creation delays and, at times, ends. The unpredictably woven embroidered artwork of worldwide stock chains disentangled, delineating the delicacy of the frameworks that support global exchange.

The assembling area endured the worst part of these interruptions. Enterprises dependent on inputs from vigorously impacted locales confronted prompt difficulties. The auto area, for example, encountered a huge lull as makers battled to get fundamental parts. The energy area, previously wrestling with changes popular and international pressures, saw a sharp decrease in oil costs as worldwide travel ground to a close stop. These interruptions flowed through the whole worth chain, influencing essential makers as well as downstream ventures and related administrations.

Exchange, a foundation of monetary reliance, experienced extreme interruptions as countries executed measures to control the infection's spread. Borders shut, ports confronted blockage, and airfreight limits reduced, prompting a sharp decrease in the volume of merchandise being moved. The World Exchange Association (WTO) extended a decrease in world product exchange of somewhere in the range of 13% and 32% in 2020, featuring the degree of the disturbance. The slump in exchange impacted both high level and creating economies, enhancing the monetary difficulties looked by countries all over the planet.

The work market arose as a point of convergence of the prompt financial aftermath, with far reaching employment misfortunes, leaves, and pay incongruities. The help area, especially businesses like cordiality, the travel industry, and diversion, encountered an unexpected and extreme constriction. Lockdowns and social separating estimates delivered numerous organizations in these areas monetarily unviable, prompting mass cutbacks and terminations. The Worldwide Work Association (ILO) assessed that functioning hours declined by 8.8% universally in 2020, identical to 255 million everyday positions.

The flying business, a basic part of worldwide network and financial action, confronted an existential emergency. With borders shut and travel limitations set up, carriers encountered a steep drop in traveler interest. Great many flights were grounded, prompting monetary misery for carriers, air terminals, and related help ventures. The effect undulated through the whole flying biological system, influencing airplane makers, support suppliers, and the travel industry subordinate economies.

The difficulties looked by little and medium-sized undertakings (SMEs) were especially intense during the underlying periods of the pandemic. Frequently working on close overall revenues and coming up short on the monetary stores of bigger enterprises, numerous SMEs confronted existential dangers.

The conclusion of organizations, disturbances in income, and restricted admittance to credit made a powerful coincidence for these substances. States all over the planet carried out different measures to help SMEs, including awards, credits, and pay sponsorships, yet the sheer size of the monetary compression stressed the adequacy of these intercessions.

Monetary business sectors experienced outrageous unpredictability as vulnerability encompassing the financial effect of the pandemic set off alarm selling and wild cost swings. Securities exchanges, when thought about indicators of monetary wellbeing, saw fast decays, with significant records encountering their steepest drops since the 2008 monetary emergency. Financial backers looked for place of refuge resources, prompting a flood popular for government bonds and gold. National banks answered by executing measures to balance out monetary business sectors, including financing cost cuts and huge liquidity infusions.

The energy area confronted a double shock from the pandemic and an oil cost battle between significant oil-delivering countries. With worldwide monetary exercises coming to a standstill, interest for oil dove. All the while, a question among Russia and Saudi Arabia prompted a surge of oil on the lookout, making costs breakdown. The oil and gas industry, previously wrestling with the drawn out change to sustainable power, confronted prompt difficulties regarding oversupply, diminished request, and monetary pressure.

The prompt financial aftermath likewise uncovered the deficiencies of social wellbeing nets in numerous nations. Laborers in casual and gig economy areas, frequently barred from conventional social assurance frameworks, confronted intense weaknesses. The absence of paid wiped out leave, medical coverage, and joblessness helps left numerous people and families without a monetary wellbeing net during a time of phenomenal financial vulnerability. The emergency revealed the requirement for complete and versatile social security systems that can answer unexpected shocks.

Legislatures overall answered with a scope of strategy measures pointed toward relieving the monetary aftermath and forestalling a total financial implosion. Financial boost bundles, intended to infuse liquidity into economies and backing organizations and people, were carried out on a remarkable scale. National banks executed money related measures, including loan fee cuts and resource buys, to settle monetary business sectors and guarantee the accessibility of credit. These strategy reactions, while significant in forestalling a more profound emergency, likewise raised worries about the drawn out results, including inflationary tensions and monetary irregular characteristics.

The prompt monetary aftermath likewise highlighted the significance of innovation in alleviating disturbances and working with financial coherence. Remote work turned into a standard for some ventures, utilizing computerized correspondence and joint effort devices. Web based business encountered a flood popular as purchasers moved towards internet shopping.

The pandemic sped up advanced change drives, compelling organizations to adjust to the new truth of virtual tasks. Be that as it may, the advanced separation turned out to be more articulated as variations in web access and computerized abilities ruined the capacity of specific populaces to adjust to the new typical.

1.2 Examination of sectors most affected and the disparities in impact

The effect of the Coronavirus pandemic has not been uniform across areas, prompting huge abberations in financial aftermath. A few businesses confronted intense difficulties, while others exhibited flexibility or even profited from the progressions in purchaser conduct and monetary elements. This assessment dives into the areas generally impacted by the pandemic and investigates the differences in influence, revealing insight into the complex and nuanced nature of the financial outcomes.

Travel and The travel industry:

The movement and the travel industry area endured the worst part of the pandemic's effect, encountering an unmatched slump as worldwide travel ground to a close stop. Carriers confronted an uncommon drop in traveler interest, prompting grounded flights, cutbacks, and monetary misery. Essentially, the neighborliness business, including inns, cafés, and diversion scenes, saw mass terminations and cutbacks as lockdowns and social separating estimates made conventional tasks illogical. The travel industry subordinate economies, especially in locales vigorously dependent on global guests, confronted serious monetary constrictions, featuring the weakness of this area to outer shocks.

Retail and Customer Merchandise:

The retail area confronted a double test, with physical stores covered during lockdowns and customer conduct moving towards online business. Conventional retail outlets, particularly those without a hearty internet based presence, attempted to adjust to the new reality. On the other side, web based business encountered a flood popular as customers, bound to their homes, went to internet looking for fundamentals and unnecessary items the same. The variations were clear inside the area, with fundamental merchandise and basic food item retailers seeing expanded request, while unnecessary retailers confronted terminations and decreased people strolling through.

Assembling and Inventory network:

The assembling area experienced disturbances in worldwide stock chains, uncovering the weakness of interconnected creation organizations. Businesses intensely dependent on inputs from districts most impacted by the pandemic confronted quick difficulties.

The auto area, for example, experienced creation delays because of deficiencies of basic parts. The disturbances undulated through the inventory network, affecting makers as well as providers, wholesalers, and retailers. The dependence on "in the nick of time" stock frameworks, pointed toward limiting costs through effective stock chains, ended up being a disadvantage during an emergency of this size.

Oil and Energy:

The energy area confronted a double shock from the pandemic and an oil cost battle between significant oil-delivering countries. With worldwide monetary exercises coming to a standstill, interest for oil plunged. All the while, a debate among Russia and Saudi Arabia prompted a surge of oil on the lookout, making costs breakdown. The oil and gas industry, previously wrestling with the drawn out change to environmentally friendly power, confronted quick difficulties regarding oversupply, decreased request, and monetary pressure. Renewables, then again, showed versatility, for certain areas encountering expanded dependence on clean energy sources during the pandemic.

Innovation:

The innovation area showed amazing flexibility during the pandemic, with numerous tech organizations encountering expanded interest for their items and administrations. Remote work turned into a standard for some enterprises, prompting a flood popular for computerized correspondence and joint effort instruments. Internet business stages flourished as buyers moved towards web based shopping. Nonetheless, the advantages of this area were not equitably disseminated. Enormous innovation organizations with vigorous computerized framework and enhanced income streams fared well, while more modest new businesses confronted difficulties, especially those in areas straightforwardly affected by lockdowns and limitations.

Medical care and Drugs:

The medical care area confronted phenomenal difficulties and valuable open doors during the pandemic. Emergency clinics and medical care offices, especially those in areas vigorously impacted by Coronavirus, experienced burdens on assets, overpowered medical services frameworks, and disturbances in elective strategies. On the other side, the drug business saw expanded interest for clinical supplies, medicines, and, most prominently, the turn of events and circulation of antibodies. Variations inside the area were apparent, with specific portions confronting monetary strain while others contributed fundamentally to pandemic reaction endeavors.

Training:

The instruction area saw significant disturbances as schools and colleges shut their actual ways to control the infection's spread. The shift to remote learning presented difficulties concerning computerized admittance, innovation foundation, and instructive value.

Differences arose as understudies from lower-pay families confronted challenges getting to online training, compounding existing imbalances in instructive results. Instructive innovation organizations experienced expanded request, however the computerized partition featured the requirement for designated endeavors to guarantee that all understudies have equivalent admittance to quality schooling.

Monetary Administrations:

The monetary area experienced outrageous unpredictability during the beginning phases of the pandemic, with securities exchanges seeing sharp decays and wild cost swings. National banks executed exceptional money related measures, including loan fee cuts and monstrous liquidity infusions, to balance out monetary business sectors. While these actions forestalled a total monetary implosion, they raised worries about the drawn out results, including likely expansion, resource bubbles, and monetary uneven characters. Inconsistencies inside the monetary area were obvious, for certain fragments profiting from market elements while others confronted difficulties.

Broadcast communications and Media:

The broadcast communications and media area assumed a critical part in working with remote work, correspondence, and diversion during the pandemic. With individuals restricted to their homes, there was expanded interest for broadband administrations, streaming stages, and computerized content. The area exhibited versatility, for certain organizations encountering development in endorser numbers and income. In any case, challenges were available, especially for conventional news sources confronting disturbances in promoting income as organizations cut showcasing spending plans in the midst of monetary vulnerability.

Land:

The land area confronted difficulties as lockdowns and monetary vulnerability impacted property markets. Business land, especially office spaces, confronted decreased request as remote work became predominant. Retail land likewise experienced hardships as terminations and changes in buyer conduct affected customary shopping spaces. On the private housing market, there were varieties, for certain locales encountering decreases in property estimations while others saw expanded interest for rural and provincial properties as people looked for additional space and less thickly populated regions.

Variations in the effect of the pandemic across areas were affected by variables like the idea of the business, computerized preparation, reliance on actual cooperations, and flexibility to remote work. While specific areas confronted intense difficulties and interruptions, others exhibited strength and versatility, displaying the different and dynamic nature of the worldwide economy. As countries explore the intricacies of recuperation, tending to these variations and encouraging a more comprehensive and practical monetary scene becomes principal.

1.3 Lessons learned from the crisis and the need for adaptive economic strategies

The Coronavirus pandemic has been a cauldron, testing the strength of countries, economies, and social orders on a worldwide scale. As the world wrestled with exceptional difficulties, a few basic examples arose, molding the story on the requirement for versatile monetary systems. This investigation digs into the key examples gained from the emergency and highlights the basic of encouraging flexibility, manageability, and inclusivity in financial systems.

Flexibility Notwithstanding Vulnerability:

The pandemic highlighted the significance of incorporating flexibility into monetary frameworks to endure unanticipated shocks. Conventional models that focused on effectiveness and cost decrease frequently generally ruled out possibilities. The emergency uncovered the requirement for organizations, supply chains, and states to embrace a stronger methodology, one that variables in the capriciousness of worldwide occasions. This involves enhancing supply chains, building monetary holds, and creating adaptable plans of action equipped for adjusting to quick changes in economic situations.

Variation to Remote Work and Advanced Change:

The quick shift to remote work featured the groundbreaking force of computerized innovations. Organizations and enterprises that had put resources into advanced framework and embraced mechanical development were better situated to adjust to the difficulties presented by lockdowns and social separating measures. The emergency filled in as an impetus for the speed increase of computerized change drives, underscoring the requirement for associations to focus on innovation as a foundation of their functional procedures. This illustration stretches out past remote work to envelop more extensive computerized preparation and flexibility notwithstanding future interruptions.

Comprehensive Financial Strategies and Social Wellbeing Nets:

The incongruities uncovered by the pandemic highlighted the significance of comprehensive monetary strategies and strong social wellbeing nets. Weak populaces, remembering casual laborers and those for dubious work, confronted uplifted gambles during the emergency. State run administrations were constrained to execute measures to help people and organizations, however the requirement for long haul arrangements became obvious. Comprehensive monetary strategies that address social imbalances, guarantee admittance to medical services and training, and give a wellbeing net to all residents arose as goals for building a strong and evenhanded society.

Worldwide Joint effort and Collaboration:

The pandemic featured the weaknesses innate in a divided worldwide reaction. The absence of facilitated worldwide endeavors in the beginning phases of the emergency highlighted the difficulties of preparing aggregate activity despite a worldwide danger. Illustrations learned stressed the requirement for improved worldwide joint effort and collaboration, especially in regions, for example, antibody dispersion, general wellbeing measures, and financial recuperation. The interconnected idea of difficulties, from environmental change to general wellbeing emergencies, requires a restored obligation to global collaboration for aggregate prosperity.

Reassessment of Worldwide Inventory Chains:

Disturbances in worldwide stock chains provoked a reassessment of customary models that focused on productivity over flexibility. The emergency exposed the dangers related with over-dependence on specific locales for basic parts. Organizations and policymakers are presently reconsidering store network techniques to upgrade their strength. This includes expanding sources, consolidating overt repetitiveness in inventory network organizations, and utilizing innovation to make more light-footed and responsive frameworks. The center is moving towards making supply anchors that are versatile to disturbances and equipped for enduring unanticipated difficulties.

Ecological Maintainability as Really important:

The brief decreases in fossil fuel byproducts and enhancements in air quality during lockdowns featured the unpredictable linkages between monetary exercises and ecological wellbeing. Illustrations learned stressed the earnestness of focusing on ecological supportability in monetary systems. States, organizations, and people are perceiving the need to decouple financial development from natural corruption. Interests in clean energy, manageable practices, and eco-accommodating advancements are becoming basic parts of monetary recuperation plans, mirroring a more extensive obligation to building a more feasible future.

Interest in General Wellbeing Foundation:

The stress on medical services frameworks during the pandemic highlighted the significance of hearty general wellbeing foundation. Examples learned accentuated the requirement for supported interest in medical services limit, innovative work, and pandemic readiness. Reinforcing medical services frameworks, both regarding actual foundation and HR, arose as a basic need. The emergency featured the interconnectedness of worldwide wellbeing, accentuating that putting resources into wellbeing at both the public and global levels is a fundamental part of financial versatility.

Adaptability in Money related and Financial Approaches:

National banks and states confronted the test of carrying out financial and monetary strategies to settle economies and forestall a total monetary implosion. Examples learned highlighted the requirement for adaptability in arrangement systems. The extraordinary idea of the emergency required whimsical measures, from loan cost slices to monstrous liquidity infusions. The capacity to adjust strategies to the one of a kind conditions of an emergency became pivotal, underlining the significance of keeping up with adaptability in monetary administration structures.

Focusing on Comprehensive Training and Computerized Proficiency:

The disturbances to schooling during the pandemic accentuated the requirement for comprehensive instructive arrangements and computerized proficiency drives. The shift to remote learning uncovered variations in admittance to schooling, especially for understudies from lower-pay families. Examples learned highlighted the significance of designated endeavors to connect the advanced gap, guaranteeing that all understudies have equivalent admittance to quality schooling. Moreover, there is an acknowledgment of the need to integrate computerized proficiency into instructive educational plans to get ready people for the developing advanced scene.

Adjusting Globalization and Public Versatility:

The pandemic incited a reexamination of globalization elements, with a restored center around accomplishing a harmony among interconnectedness and public versatility. While globalization has brought monetary advantages, the emergency uncovered weaknesses related with over-reliance on outside hotspots for basic assets. Examples learned underlined the significance of finding some kind of harmony that tackles the benefits of globalization while guaranteeing that countries have the ability to answer autonomously to emergencies, encouraging both worldwide participation and public strength.

Chapter 2

Policy Responses and Stimulus Measures

The Coronavirus pandemic has been a pot, testing the versatility of countries, economies, and social orders on a worldwide scale. As the world wrestled with uncommon difficulties, a few basic illustrations arose, molding the story on the requirement for versatile monetary techniques. This investigation digs into the key illustrations gained from the emergency and highlights the basic of cultivating versatility, maintainability, and inclusivity in monetary structures.

Strength Despite Vulnerability:

The pandemic highlighted the significance of incorporating strength into financial frameworks to endure unexpected shocks. Customary models that focused on effectiveness and cost decrease frequently pretty much ruled out possibilities. The emergency uncovered the requirement for organizations, supply chains, and legislatures to embrace a stronger methodology, one that elements in the eccentricism of worldwide occasions. This involves enhancing supply chains, building monetary saves, and creating adaptable plans of action fit for adjusting to fast changes in economic situations.

Variation to Remote Work and Advanced Change:

The fast shift to remote work featured the extraordinary force of advanced innovations. Organizations and enterprises that had put resources into computerized framework and embraced mechanical advancement were better situated to adjust to the difficulties presented by lockdowns and social separating measures. The emergency filled in as an impetus for the speed increase of computerized change drives, underscoring the requirement for associations to focus on innovation as a foundation of their functional methodologies. This illustration reaches out past remote work to envelop more extensive computerized preparation and versatility despite future disturbances.

Comprehensive Monetary Arrangements and Social Wellbeing Nets:

The abberations exposed by the pandemic highlighted the significance of comprehensive financial approaches and powerful friendly security nets. Weak populaces, remembering casual laborers and those for unstable business, confronted elevated takes a chance during the emergency. States were constrained to carry out measures to help people and organizations, yet the requirement for long haul arrangements became apparent. Comprehensive financial strategies that address social imbalances, guarantee admittance to medical services and schooling, and give a wellbeing net to all residents arose as goals for building a versatile and evenhanded society.

Worldwide Joint effort and Participation:

The pandemic featured the weaknesses innate in a divided worldwide reaction. The absence of facilitated worldwide endeavors in the beginning phases of the emergency highlighted the difficulties of preparing aggregate activity even with a worldwide danger. Examples learned underscored the requirement for upgraded worldwide coordinated effort and participation, especially in regions, for example, immunization circulation, general wellbeing measures, and financial recuperation. The interconnected idea of difficulties, from environmental change to general wellbeing emergencies, requires a reestablished obligation to worldwide collaboration for aggregate prosperity.

Reassessment of Worldwide Inventory Chains:

Disturbances in worldwide stock chains provoked a reassessment of conventional models that focused on productivity over flexibility. The emergency exposed the dangers related with over-dependence on specific districts for basic parts. Organizations and policymakers are currently rethinking inventory network techniques to improve their versatility. This includes enhancing sources, consolidating overt repetitiveness in production network organizations, and utilizing innovation to make more spry and responsive frameworks. The center is moving towards making supply anchors that are versatile to interruptions and fit for enduring unexpected difficulties.

Ecological Manageability as Really important:

The brief decreases in fossil fuel byproducts and upgrades in air quality during lockdowns featured the complex linkages between monetary exercises and ecological wellbeing. Illustrations learned accentuated the earnestness of focusing on ecological manageability in financial techniques. States, organizations, and people are perceiving the need to decouple monetary development from natural corruption. Interests in clean energy, supportable practices, and eco-accommodating advances are becoming fundamental parts of monetary recuperation plans, mirroring a more extensive obligation to building a more feasible future.

Interest in General Wellbeing Framework:

The stress on medical services frameworks during the pandemic highlighted the significance of vigorous general wellbeing foundation. Examples learned underlined the requirement for supported interest in medical care limit, innovative work, and pandemic readiness. Reinforcing medical care frameworks, both with regards to actual foundation and HR, arose as a basic need. The emergency featured the interconnectedness of worldwide wellbeing, accentuating that putting resources into wellbeing at both the public and global levels is a fundamental part of monetary strength.

Adaptability in Money related and Financial Arrangements:

National banks and states confronted the test of carrying out financial and monetary strategies to balance out economies and forestall a total financial implosion.

Illustrations learned highlighted the requirement for adaptability in approach structures. The uncommon idea of the emergency required whimsical measures, from loan fee slices to enormous liquidity infusions. The capacity to adjust strategies to the special conditions of an emergency became pivotal, stressing the significance of keeping up with adaptability in financial administration structures.

Focusing on Comprehensive Instruction and Computerized Proficiency:

The disturbances to schooling during the pandemic accentuated the requirement for comprehensive instructive strategies and advanced education drives. The shift to remote learning exposed variations in admittance to schooling, especially for understudies from lower-pay families. Illustrations learned highlighted the significance of designated endeavors to connect the advanced separation, guaranteeing that all understudies have equivalent admittance to quality schooling. Moreover, there is an acknowledgment of the need to integrate computerized proficiency into instructive educational plans to get ready people for the developing advanced scene.

Adjusting Globalization and Public Flexibility:

The pandemic provoked a reexamination of globalization elements, with a reestablished center around accomplishing a harmony among interconnectedness and public versatility. While globalization has brought financial advantages, the emergency uncovered weaknesses related with over-reliance on outside hotspots for basic assets.

Illustrations learned underlined the significance of finding some kind of harmony that outfits the upsides of globalization while guaranteeing that countries have the ability to answer freely to emergencies, encouraging both worldwide collaboration and public flexibility.

2.1 Assessment of government interventions and fiscal policies worldwide

The worldwide reaction to the financial difficulties presented by the Coronavirus pandemic has been set apart by a variety of government intercessions and monetary strategies pointed toward balancing out economies, supporting organizations and people, and establishing the groundwork for recuperation. This evaluation investigates the assorted methodologies utilized by legislatures around the world, featuring the victories, difficulties, and ramifications of these mediations.

Uncommon Financial Boost:

State run administrations answered the financial aftermath from the pandemic with unmatched monetary upgrade measures. The size of financial mediations was notable, with numerous countries committing trillions of dollars to help their economies. These improvement bundles enveloped a scope of measures, including direct money moves, awards and credits to organizations, and interests in basic areas like medical care and foundation.

The prompt effect of financial upgrade was obvious in forestalling a more extreme monetary constriction. Cash moves gave truly necessary help to people confronting pay misfortunes, and business support programs meant to forestall far and wide terminations and employment misfortunes. Notwithstanding, the adequacy of financial upgrade fluctuated across nations, with variables like the speed of execution, the designated idea of measures, and the generally monetary setting affecting results.

Financial Approach Reactions:

National banks assumed a significant part in settling monetary business sectors and guaranteeing the accessibility of credit during the emergency. Money related strategy reactions included loan fee cuts, resource buys, and liquidity infusions. National banks, including the Central bank, the European National Bank, and the Bank of Japan, executed measures to bring down financing costs, giving ideal getting conditions to organizations and families.

The outcome of money related strategy mediations in animating financial action confronted difficulties as loan costs drew nearer or arrived at the zero lower bound in numerous economies. While these actions forestalled a monetary implosion and guaranteed liquidity, concerns arose about possible secondary effects, including resource bubbles and monetary uneven characters.

The drawn out ramifications of far reaching money related strategies stayed a subject of continuous discussion among financial specialists and policymakers.

Support for Organizations and Business:

Perceiving the serious disturbances looked by organizations, legislatures executed a scope of measures to offer monetary help and safeguard work. These drives included awards, credits, charge alleviation, and pay sponsorships. The goal was to forestall boundless terminations, empower organizations to climate the quick emergency, and keep away from an extended ascent in joblessness.

The progress of business support estimates relied upon variables like the flexibility of organizations, the term of the emergency, and the viability of execution. While these actions forestalled a more critical monetary slump, challenges arose in arriving at specific areas, particularly those vigorously affected by lockdowns and limitations. The drawn out feasibility of organizations and the potential for primary changes in specific enterprises became central marks of conversation.

Social Security Nets and Joblessness Advantages:

The ascent in joblessness provoked states to upgrade social security nets and joblessness benefits. Extended and extra advantages meant to offer monetary help to people and families confronting employment misfortunes. The goal was to forestall a sharp expansion in destitution rates, guarantee admittance to fundamental assets, and address the quick requirements of weak populaces.

The difficulties in executing compelling social security nets included coming to casual and gig economy laborers, guaranteeing quick payment of assets, and forestalling possible holes in inclusion. The pandemic featured the requirement for powerful friendly security nets fit for answering unexpected monetary shocks and guaranteeing the prosperity, everything being equal.

Obligation Help Drives:

Elevated degrees of obligation, especially in emerging nations, provoked worldwide organizations and a few states to present obligation help drives. These drives meant to lighten the obligation trouble, permitting countries to divert assets towards fundamental public administrations and monetary recuperation. Obligation bans, concessional funding, and obligation rebuilding measures were among the instruments utilized to give alleviation to nations confronting monetary limitations.

The progress of obligation help drives relied on the collaboration of banks, including both two-sided and multilateral loan specialists. While these actions gave transitory help, concerns endured about the drawn out financial supportability of nations and the possible effect on their FICO assessments. The requirement for a planned and extensive way to deal with obligation help stayed a point of convergence of conversations among global monetary foundations and benefactor nations.

Green Recuperation and Reasonable Ventures:

A states jumping all over the chance to adjust financial recuperation endeavors to natural manageability objectives. Green recuperation drives remembered ventures for environmentally friendly power, energy-productive foundation, and economical innovations. The objective was not exclusively to invigorate financial movement yet in addition to speed up the change to a more maintainable and low-carbon future.

The outcome of green recuperation drives relied upon variables, for example, the prioritization of economical ventures, the coordination of ecological contemplations into policymaking, and public help for green drives. Challenges arose in adjusting momentary monetary needs with long haul supportability objectives and guaranteeing that green recuperation measures added to work creation and financial development.

Support for Little and Medium-Sized Endeavors (SMEs):

Perceiving the crucial job of little and medium-sized ventures (SMEs) in economies around the world, legislatures executed designated measures to help these organizations. Programs included awards, advances, and help with functional difficulties like lease and utilities. The goal was to forestall far reaching terminations, safeguard occupations, and keep up with the variety and dynamism of the business biological system.

The outcome of SME support estimates depended on variables, for example, the availability of subsidizing, the proficiency of use processes, and the length of the emergency. Challenges emerged in coming to the most weak SMEs, especially those in casual areas or lacking advanced framework. The pandemic featured the requirement for long haul procedures to upgrade the versatility of SMEs and encourage a climate helpful for their development.

Advanced Change and Development Backing:

The pandemic sped up computerized change across ventures, inciting a few legislatures to help development and innovation reception. Measures included subsidizing for innovative work, support for computerized framework ventures, and drives to improve advanced education. The objective was to situate economies for the future by cultivating development, adjusting to changing customer ways of behaving, and tackling the groundbreaking force of innovation.

Challenges in supporting advanced change drives remembered tending to variations for computerized admittance, guaranteeing network protection, and relieving potential work removal because of computerization. The pandemic highlighted the significance of an essential way to deal with computerized change, stressing both the valuable open doors and difficulties related with mechanical development.

Worldwide Participation in Antibody Dispersion:

As immunizations turned into a pivotal device in dealing with the pandemic, worldwide participation arose as a key subject. Drives, for example, COVAX expected to guarantee evenhanded admittance to immunizations around the world, no matter what a country's monetary status. Contributor countries, worldwide associations, and drug organizations teamed up to work with immunization creation, dissemination, and access, it was interconnected to perceive that worldwide wellbeing security.

Challenges in worldwide antibody dissemination included strategic intricacies, international strains, and variations in immunization accessibility. Examples learned underscored the requirement for supported participation, the significance of multi-lateral foundations, and the acknowledgment that tending to worldwide wellbeing challenges requires aggregate endeavors.

Tending to Imbalance and Social Shameful acts:

The pandemic exacerbated existing social disparities and treacheries, inciting conversations about the requirement for strategy reactions that address foundational issues. A few states acquainted measures with tackle disparity, including charge changes, social projects, and drives to advance comprehensive monetary development. The objective was to guarantee that the recuperation interaction was evenhanded, with benefits arriving at all fragments of society.

Challenges in tending to imbalance incorporated the requirement for supported endeavors, expected protection from primary changes, and the mind boggling transaction of monetary, social, and political variables. The pandemic highlighted the significance of addressing basic variations to fabricate a stronger and comprehensive financial establishment.

2.2 Successful policy implementations

The progress of strategy executions, especially with regards to the Coronavirus pandemic, has been a basic determinant of how countries endured the hardship, safeguarded their economies, and set up for recuperation. This evaluation investigates occurrences of fruitful approach executions across different aspects, featuring techniques that demonstrated successful in alleviating the prompt effect of the emergency and encouraging strength.

Quick and Conclusive Reactions:

Countries that answered quickly and conclusively to the arising emergency showed a more serious level of outcome in containing the financial aftermath. Nations like New Zealand, Taiwan, and South Korea executed early and severe measures, including boundless testing, contact following, and lockdowns, really checking the spread of the infection. This approach safeguarded general wellbeing as well as established the groundwork for a speedier monetary bounce back. Quick reactions permitted these countries to contain the infection, limit interruptions, and position themselves for a quicker return to predictability.

Powerful Correspondence and Public Trust:

Fruitful strategy executions were much of the time joined by compelling correspondence procedures that encouraged public trust and consistence. Pioneers who conveyed straightforwardly, gave clear rules, and participated in ordinary updates acquired the trust of their populaces. This trust was instrumental in guaranteeing public consistence with wellbeing and security measures, working with the execution of lockdowns and social removing conventions. Nations like Germany, under Chancellor Angela Merkel's administration, exemplified viable correspondence, bringing about boundless adherence to preventive measures and a somewhat lower financial effect.

Designated Help for Weak Populaces:

Approaches that designated help towards weak populaces, remembering low-pay people and those for tricky business, exhibited adequacy in alleviating the social and monetary effect of the pandemic. Measures, for example, direct money moves, extended joblessness advantages, and food help programs gave a security net to those generally impacted. Nations like Canada and Australia executed powerful friendly help programs, offering monetary help to people and organizations in a designated way, which added to social soundness and forestalled a sharp ascent in neediness rates.

Adaptability and Flexibility in Strategy Approaches:

Effective strategy executions showed adaptability and flexibility, perceiving the developing idea of the emergency. States that changed their systems because of evolving conditions, new variations of the infection, and arising monetary difficulties exhibited versatility. For example, Singapore carried out a "electrical switch" approach and adjusted control estimates in light of continuous information, taking into account a harmony between general wellbeing and financial contemplations. This flexibility empowered these countries to explore vulnerabilities and designer reactions to the extraordinary elements of the emergency.

Coordination Among Financial and Money related Approaches:

Nations that successfully planned financial and money related strategies showed a more vigorous reaction to the monetary difficulties.

National banks working pair with monetary specialists gave liquidity support, brought down loan costs, and carried out measures to settle monetary business sectors. This coordination, frequently alluded to as "strategy blend," was clear in the reaction of the US, where the Central bank carried out money related measures while the public authority passed significant monetary upgrade bundles. This synchronized methodology forestalled a monetary emergency and upheld financial recuperation.

Interest in Medical services Foundation and Exploration:

Countries that focused on interests in medical care framework and exploration displayed an essential way to deal with emergency the board. Nations like South Korea and Germany had solid medical services frameworks with far and wide testing abilities, productive contact following, and adequate medical care limit. Also, proactive interests in immunization exploration, advancement, and assembling limit added to their capacity to carry out inoculation crusades quickly. This essential interest in medical services framework situated these countries for powerful pandemic administration and sped up recuperation.

Support for Advanced Change and Remote Work:

Arrangements that upheld advanced change and worked with remote work added to monetary flexibility during lockdowns. Nations like Finland and the Netherlands had vigorous advanced foundation and arrangements that advanced remote work, permitting specific areas to proceed with activities. This approach alleviated disturbances in monetary exercises and empowered organizations to adjust to new working circumstances. Legislatures that put resources into computerized education programs and upheld innovation reception showed prescience in exploring the difficulties presented by the pandemic.

Worldwide Participation and Fortitude:

Outcome in dealing with the pandemic frequently elaborate worldwide participation and fortitude. Nations that effectively taken part in worldwide joint efforts for immunization circulation, data sharing, and facilitated reactions showed initiative in tending to a worldwide emergency. The COVAX drive, upheld by various countries and associations, exemplified an endeavor to guarantee fair admittance to immunizations around the world. Pioneers who underlined the interconnectedness of worldwide wellbeing and the significance of aggregate activity added to a more compelling and composed worldwide reaction.

Green Recuperation Drives:

A countries utilized the emergency as a chance to adjust financial recuperation endeavors to maintainability objectives. Green recuperation drives, remembering speculations for environmentally friendly power, practical foundation, and eco-accommodating advancements, invigorated financial movement as well as tended to long haul natural difficulties. Nations like Norway and New Zealand integrated green drives into their recuperation plans, displaying a guarantee to building an additional reasonable and strong future.

Local area Commitment and Granular perspectives:

Effective arrangements frequently elaborate local area commitment and granular perspectives that utilized neighborhood information and assets. Nations that enabled neighborhood networks, enrolled their collaboration in carrying out preventive measures, and used grassroots organizations were better ready to deal with the emergency. The progress of nations like Japan in containing the infection was credited, to a limited extent, to a culture of veil wearing, adherence to cleanliness practices, and local area driven endeavors to check the spread.

Commonsense Testing and Immunization Procedures:

Commonsense testing and immunization systems assumed a critical part in dealing with the pandemic. Nations like Israel and the Unified Realm executed forceful immunization crusades, accomplishing high inoculation rates in a generally brief period.

These missions, combined with designated testing and contact following, added to the regulation of the infection and made ready for a more sped up return to monetary predictability.

Versatility in Monetary Enhancement:

Economies that displayed strength through broadening systems were better prepared to endure the hardship. Nations like the Unified Bedouin Emirates (UAE) and Singapore, with enhanced economies spreading over numerous areas, exhibited the capacity to turn and adjust to changing monetary circumstances. Broadening gave a support against the effect on unambiguous enterprises, permitting these countries to keep up with monetary dependability.

2.3 Critique of potential shortcomings and long-term implications

The reaction to the Coronavirus pandemic, while set apart by prominent accomplishments in approach executions, has additionally confronted huge scrutinizes and presents long haul suggestions that merit cautious thought. This study investigates likely deficiencies in the worldwide reaction and digs into the expansive outcomes that might shape the post-pandemic world.

Discriminatory Admittance to Antibodies:

One of the most incredibly glaring deficiencies of the worldwide reaction to the pandemic has been the glaring imbalances in antibody dissemination. While a few created countries quickly got and regulated immunizations to a huge piece of their populaces, many non-industrial nations battled to get to a sufficient stock. The worldwide immunization circulation has featured the split among princely and asset compelled countries, compounding existing wellbeing inconsistencies. This disparity acts moral worries like well as has ramifications for the delayed span of the pandemic, as uncontrolled episodes in specific districts can prompt the development of new variations that might affect worldwide endeavors to accomplish group resistance.

Immunization Patriotism and Storing:

The peculiarity of immunization patriotism, where nations focus on getting antibodies for their own populaces to the detriment of evenhanded dispersion, has obstructed worldwide endeavors to accomplish broad invulnerability. A few countries participated in immunization storing, marking bargains for additional portions than required and restricting the accessibility of immunizations for different nations. This approach worsens worldwide imbalances as well as subverts the standard of fortitude in tending to a worldwide wellbeing emergency. The potential long haul result is a broken worldwide local area, upsetting cooperative endeavors to address future worldwide difficulties.

Divided Global Collaboration:

The pandemic uncovered the difficulties of accomplishing facilitated worldwide reactions. While some participation endeavors, like the COVAX drive, meant to give impartial admittance to antibodies, international pressures and immunization patriotism stressed worldwide cooperation. The absence of a brought together worldwide technique in the beginning phases of the pandemic added to postpones in data sharing, lopsided dissemination of clinical assets, and differed strategy reactions. The drawn out suggestion is a requirement for reinforced worldwide administration designs and systems to address wellbeing emergencies as well as other transnational difficulties.

Monetary Differences and Recuperation:

The monetary aftermath from the pandemic has excessively impacted specific areas and socioeconomics. While certain enterprises experienced development, others, like accommodation and the travel industry, confronted serious difficulties. Moreover, minimized networks and weak populaces bore a lopsided weight of the monetary effect. The scrutinize lies in the lopsided idea of recuperation, where certain fragments of the populace and businesses might battle to recover pre-pandemic degrees of dependability. This monetary dissimilarity might propagate social imbalances, presenting long haul difficulties for comprehensive financial development.

Obligation Weight and Monetary Maintainability:

The broad monetary boost measures sent by states universally have prompted a flood in open obligation. While these actions were fundamental for forestalling monetary breakdown, the drawn out ramifications of uplifted obligation levels raise worries about financial supportability. Nations, especially those in the creating scene, face the test of overseeing raised obligation loads, possibly compelling their capacity to put resources into fundamental public administrations, foundation, and practical turn of events. Finding some kind of harmony between tending to quick financial difficulties and guaranteeing long haul monetary manageability is a sensitive undertaking that requires cautious thought.

Influence on Psychological wellness and Prosperity:

The pandemic has negatively affected psychological wellness and prosperity all around the world. Delayed lockdowns, monetary vulnerabilities, and disturbances to day to day existence have added to expanded degrees of stress, tension, and sadness. The scrutinize lies in the deficiency of psychological well-being emotionally supportive networks, as numerous nations confronted difficulties in satisfying the developing need for emotional wellness administrations. The drawn out suggestions incorporate a potential psychological well-being emergency, requiring supported endeavors to de-stigmatize emotional wellness, extend admittance to administrations, and focus on mental prosperity as a general wellbeing need.

Instruction Disturbances and Learning Disparities:

The conclusion of schools and disturbances to training have broadened learning disparities, especially for understudies in low-pay and underestimated networks. The shift to remote learning uncovered abberations in admittance to innovation and advanced proficiency. The scrutinize fixates on the absence of an exhaustive and generally pertinent system for guaranteeing proceeded with schooling during emergencies. The drawn out results incorporate a likely age of understudies with lopsided instructive fulfillment, worsening existing imbalances and influencing future labor force capacities.

Store network Weaknesses:

The pandemic uncovered weaknesses in worldwide stockpile chains, especially in basic areas like medical services and innovation. Reliance on a predetermined number of providers and disturbances to transportation networks featured the delicacy of these chains. The evaluate focuses on the requirement for stronger and broadened inventory network methodologies to alleviate the dangers of future disturbances. The drawn out suggestion is a reexamination of worldwide exchange rehearses and a shift towards more decentralized and versatile store network models.

Falsehood and Disintegration of Trust:

The pervasiveness of deception and the disintegration of public confidence in organizations have been huge difficulties during the pandemic. The spread of misleading data connected with the infection, antibodies, and general wellbeing measures has ruined endeavors to control the spread of the infection and advance immunization. The study lies in the deficient systems for countering deception and reconstructing trust. The drawn out suggestions incorporate the requirement for strong correspondence procedures, interest in general wellbeing training, and endeavors to modify trust in science and public establishments.

Environment Activity Difficulties:

The earnestness of answering the quick emergency has redirected consideration and assets from tending to long haul difficulties, for example, environmental change.

While certain countries consolidated green recuperation drives, others confronted difficulties in their environment activity plans. The study is fixated on the gamble of deprioritizing ecological supportability chasing transient financial recuperation. The drawn out results might incorporate botched open doors for moderating the effects of environmental change and cultivating a more supportable future.

Innovation Driven Disparities:

The sped up reception of innovation during the pandemic has exacerbated existing disparities connected with advanced admittance and abilities. The shift to remote work and online administrations featured abberations in mechanical framework and computerized education. The scrutinize centers around the likely propagation of innovation driven imbalances, with specific populaces and locales being abandoned. The drawn out suggestion is a requirement for purposeful endeavors to connect the computerized partition and guarantee that mechanical progressions add to comprehensive financial development.

Disintegration of Vote based Standards:

A few states executed crisis estimates because of the pandemic, prompting worries about the disintegration of popularity based standards and standards. The utilization of crisis powers and limitations on common freedoms for the sake of general wellbeing brought up issues about the harmony between emergency reaction and protecting vote based values. The scrutinize focuses on the likely long haul suggestions for vote based administration, accentuating the requirement for carefulness in protecting majority rule organizations and standards.

Chapter 3

The Role of International Cooperation

The job of worldwide participation has been essential in tending to the complex difficulties presented by the Coronavirus pandemic. This extensive assessment digs into the different components of worldwide collaboration, featuring its significance in general wellbeing, financial recuperation, and the more extensive worldwide reaction.

1. **Worldwide General Wellbeing Reaction:**
   The quick spread of the infection across borders required an organized worldwide work to battle the pandemic. Associations like the World Wellbeing Association (WHO) assumed a focal part in working with data sharing, organizing research, and giving direction to nations. The sharing of logical information, best practices, and encounters from various districts empowered a more educated and successful general wellbeing reaction.
   Global collaboration was especially clear in the turn of events and circulation of antibodies. Drives like COVAX, a worldwide immunization sharing project, intended to guarantee evenhanded admittance to antibodies around the world. Benefactor nations, charitable associations, and immunization makers teamed up to speed up immunization creation and dispersion, perceiving that accomplishing worldwide wellbeing security required an aggregate methodology.
   Be that as it may, challenges arose, including antibody patriotism, biased conveyance, and store network imperatives. The pandemic highlighted the requirement for reinforced worldwide components to improve readiness, reaction, and impartial admittance to clinical assets even with worldwide wellbeing emergencies.

2. **Monetary Adjustment and Recuperation:**
   The monetary repercussions of the pandemic rose above public boundaries, requiring facilitated global endeavors to settle economies and backing recuperation. The Global Money related Asset (IMF) and World Bank assumed critical parts in giving monetary help to nations confronting financial difficulties. Obligation help drives were acquainted with mitigate the weight on agricultural

countries wrestling with elevated degrees of obligation.

Multilateral gatherings, like the G7 and G20, assembled to examine and organize monetary arrangements. The significance of cooperation was apparent in the execution of financial boost measures, money related approaches, and exchange help endeavors. Nations participated in exchange to forestall protectionist gauges and advance a more comprehensive and supportable worldwide monetary recuperation.

Be that as it may, reactions emerged in regards to the sufficiency of help for non-industrial countries and the absence of a planned worldwide financial reaction. Tending to the monetary aftermath required a more exhaustive and evenhanded methodology, underlining the interconnectedness of public economies and the basic of shared liability.

3. **Store network Flexibility and Exchange Participation:**
   The pandemic uncovered weaknesses in worldwide stockpile chains, disturbing the progression of products and fundamental clinical supplies. Worldwide participation became fundamental in tending to these difficulties and guaranteeing the strength of supply chains. Nations cooperated to work with the development of merchandise, eliminate exchange hindrances, and stay away from trade limitations on basic clinical hardware.

   Endeavors to upgrade inventory network versatility included broadening wellsprings of creation and teaming up on innovation and development. The acknowledgment that interconnected inventory chains require an aggregate methodology prompted conversations on making stronger and versatile exchange frameworks. The significance of open and unsurprising exchange was underscored for the purpose of advancing worldwide monetary recuperation.

   Nonetheless, concerns were raised about the expected ascent of protectionism and the requirement for a more comprehensive way to deal with exchange. Finding some kind of harmony between guaranteeing public safety and encouraging global participation in exchange arose as a complicated test that necessary supported discourse and coordinated effort.

4. **Logical Coordinated effort and Exploration:**
   Logical coordinated effort assumed a crucial part in figuring out the infection, creating diagnostics, medicines, and immunizations, and sharing information to further develop worldwide reaction methodologies. Specialists and researchers overall worked together on an uncommon scale, sharing information, leading joint investigations, and on the whole propelling comprehension we might interpret the infection and its variations.

   Worldwide participation in research was obvious in drives like the Admittance to Coronavirus Apparatuses (ACT) Gas pedal, which planned to speed up the turn of events, creation, and fair admittance to Coronavirus tests, medicines, and antibodies. The open sharing of examination discoveries and the obligation to making logical progressions a worldwide public great were fundamental in tending to the general wellbeing emergency.

Notwithstanding, challenges emerged in guaranteeing that the advantages of logical progressions were open to all. Issues of protected innovation, antibody creation limit, and innovation move became basic marks of conversation. Finding some kind of harmony between boosting development and guaranteeing fair admittance to life-saving advancements turned into a point of convergence in the continuous talk on the job of worldwide participation in logical exploration.

5. **Philanthropic Help and Worldwide Fortitude:**

The pandemic heightened existing helpful difficulties, with weak populaces confronting expanded difficulties. Worldwide participation assumed a urgent part in conveying helpful help, giving clinical guide, and tending to the necessities of outcasts and uprooted people. Associations like the Unified Countries High Magistrate for Outcasts (UNHCR) and non-administrative associations (NGOs) teamed up to guarantee that the most defenseless were not abandoned. Worldwide fortitude turned into a mobilizing cry, underscoring the interconnectedness of human predeterminations. Nations, associations, and people added to worldwide aid projects, perceiving that conquering the pandemic required an aggregate exertion. Drives like the World Wellbeing Gathering's goal on worldwide admittance to immunizations highlighted the obligation to abandoning nobody in the mission for a better and safer world.

Notwithstanding, scrutinizes arose in regards to the sufficiency of philanthropic help and the requirement for a more precise and composed approach. The pandemic featured the significance of building strong wellbeing frameworks and addressing fundamental social and financial disparities to guarantee a more viable and fair reaction to future emergencies.

6. **Illustrations Learned and Regions for Development:**

While worldwide collaboration demonstrated instrumental in different parts of tending to the pandemic, examples learned highlight regions for development. The requirement for a more planned and proactive worldwide reaction component was obvious, underscoring the significance of early advance notice frameworks, information sharing, and fast organization of assets notwithstanding arising wellbeing dangers.

The job of worldwide associations in working with participation and coordination was avowed yet additionally uncovered regions for change and reinforcing. Calls for changing the WHO to upgrade its ability, freedom, and adequacy acquired conspicuousness. Furthermore, conversations on the foundation of a worldwide wellbeing chamber or settlement to address future pandemics mirrored the acknowledgment that a more powerful global administration system was required.

Challenges in immunization conveyance highlighted the requirement for a more impartial and comprehensive way to deal with worldwide wellbeing. Calls for deferring protected innovation privileges on Coronavirus immunizations built up momentum, featuring the pressure between restrictive interests and the basic to guarantee wide and reasonable admittance to life-saving advances. The pandemic incited a reconsideration of the worldwide administration of wellbeing, with an emphasis on decency, value, and fortitude.

In the monetary domain, the pandemic uncovered the restrictions of existing global monetary designs to answer emergencies sufficiently. Requires "Another Bretton Woods" or an extensive change of worldwide monetary foundations got some decent forward momentum, with an accentuation on making a more comprehensive and supportable worldwide financial design.

The significance of tending to social determinants of wellbeing and building strong wellbeing frameworks turned into a focal subject in post-pandemic reflections. The pandemic highlighted the interconnectedness of wellbeing, financial prosperity, and social soundness, requiring a comprehensive way to deal with worldwide difficulties. Worldwide collaboration ought to stretch out past emergency reaction to address the main drivers of weakness and disparity.

7. International Contemplations and Future Situations:

The international scene during the pandemic was set apart by both collaboration and rivalry. While nations worked together on immunization advancement and dispersion, international pressures persevered, impacting the circulation of clinical supplies, data sharing, and the generally worldwide reaction.

Future situations imagine an existence where global collaboration turns out to be significantly more basic, with countries perceiving the common difficulties and interconnected chances. The pandemic featured the requirement for a shift from a simply serious way to deal with a more cooperative and helpful outlook in tending to worldwide difficulties.

In any case, challenges persevere, and the international scene stays complex. The potential for antibody strategy, mechanical rivalry, and disparate public interests might keep on impacting global collaboration. Finding some kind of harmony between public interests and aggregate prosperity stays a sensitive errand, requiring strategic expertise, viable multilateralism, and a promise to shared values.

3.1 Exploration of collaborative efforts among nations and global institutions

The investigation of cooperative endeavors among countries and worldwide foundations during the Coronavirus pandemic uncovers a mind boggling embroidery of participation, difficulties, and examples learned. This exhaustive assessment dives into different elements of worldwide cooperation, going from general wellbeing drives to monetary recuperation, logical examination, and philanthropic endeavors.

1. **Worldwide General Wellbeing Drives:**
   The cooperative endeavors in general wellbeing have been exemplified by drives driven by global associations like the World Wellbeing Association (WHO)

and cooperative stages like the Admittance to Coronavirus Devices (ACT) Gas pedal. These drives intended to work with fair admittance to diagnostics, medicines, and immunizations, perceiving the worldwide idea of the wellbeing emergency.

The COVAX drive, a cooperation between WHO, Gavi, the Immunization Partnership, and the Alliance for Scourge Readiness Developments (CEPI), looked to guarantee fair and opportune admittance to antibodies for all nations. Be that as it may, challenges arose in antibody appropriation, production network planned operations, and immunization patriotism, featuring the requirement for additional powerful systems to altogether address worldwide wellbeing crises.

Cooperative examination endeavors under the Fortitude Preliminary and other joint endeavors sped up the ID of viable medicines and treatments. The sharing of logical information, clinical preliminary outcomes, and best practices encouraged an aggregate way to deal with understanding and dealing with the infection. Nonetheless, examples gained from the lopsided worldwide immunization circulation highlighted the significance of tending to primary imbalances in worldwide wellbeing frameworks.

2. **Monetary Recuperation and Multilateral Collaboration:**
   The monetary aftermath from the pandemic required phenomenal degrees of cooperation in conceiving methodologies for recuperation. Multilateral gatherings, for example, the G7 and G20 assumed pivotal parts in planning monetary arrangements and monetary help. Establishments like the Global Money related Asset (IMF) and the World Bank gave monetary help, and obligation alleviation drives were acquainted with lighten the financial weight on emerging countries. In any case, differences in the degree of help gave and worries about the ampleness of the reaction featured the requirement for more comprehensive financial participation. The pandemic highlighted the interconnectedness of worldwide economies, stressing the significance of aggregate activity to forestall an extended worldwide downturn. The job of worldwide foundations in advancing fair monetary practices and forestalling protectionist measures turned into a focal concentration in molding a stronger and comprehensive financial request.

3. **Logical Cooperation and Development:**
   Logical cooperation saw a phenomenal flood during the pandemic, with specialists and researchers across borders uniting to grasp, battle, and relieve the effect of the infection. Cooperative examination stages, open-access distributing, and joint clinical preliminaries worked with the fast improvement of diagnostics, medicines, and immunizations.

   The development of variations of the infection provoked continuous global joint effort in observing and grasping the advancing danger. The recognizable proof of variations, their transmission elements, and the viability of existing antibodies became shared attempts. Be that as it may, moves in impartial admittance to explore discoveries, issues of licensed innovation privileges, and worries about the commercialization of logical information brought up issues about the eventual fate of open logical joint effort.

Advancement centers and cooperative organizations arose to address innovative difficulties, like the improvement of new diagnostics, helpful specialists, and computerized wellbeing arrangements. The cooperative soul in established researchers exhibited the potential for saddling aggregate knowledge to address worldwide wellbeing emergencies.

4. **Store network Versatility and Exchange Participation:**

   The pandemic uncovered weaknesses in worldwide stock chains, prompting disturbances in the creation and circulation of fundamental products, including clinical supplies. Cooperative endeavors planned to improve store network flexibility, expand wellsprings of creation, and eliminate exchange hindrances that blocked the progression of basic products.

   Worldwide participation became pivotal in guaranteeing the accessibility of clinical hardware, individual defensive gear (PPE), and immunizations. Discourse in multilateral gatherings stressed the requirement for unsurprising and open exchange to help worldwide financial recuperation. Notwithstanding, international strains and worries about the essential control of distinct advantages featured the sensitive harmony between cooperative exchange practices and public safety contemplations.

   The investigation of tough and reasonable store network models turned into a need, underscoring the requirement for global cooperation in upgrading the vigor of basic stock chains. Conversations fixated on the job of worldwide administration components in advancing fair exchange practices and decreasing weaknesses interconnected supply organizations.

5. **Compassionate Help and Worldwide Fortitude:**

   Philanthropic endeavors during the pandemic exemplified the force of worldwide fortitude. Associations like the Assembled Countries (UN) and non-legislative associations (NGOs) teamed up to give compassionate help, clinical guide, and backing to weak populaces. The worldwide local area mobilized to address the necessities of exiles and inside dislodged people, perceiving that the effect of the pandemic stretched out past public lines.

   Drives like the COVAX Office pointed not exclusively to give antibodies yet additionally to guarantee that low-pay nations had evenhanded admittance to these life-saving assets. Notwithstanding, challenges in financing, calculated intricacies, and international contemplations presented obstacles to the viable execution of helpful help programs.

   Worldwide fortitude turned into a characterizing element of the reaction to the pandemic, underscoring the common obligation of countries and associations in tending to the requirements of the most helpless. The investigation of cooperative endeavors in helpful help shed light on the requirement for supported obligation to standards of sympathy, compassion, and inclusivity in worldwide emergency reaction.

6. **Illustrations Learned and Difficulties:**

The cooperative endeavors among countries and worldwide establishments during the pandemic yielded important illustrations and uncovered difficulties that need cautious thought.

Illustrations learned incorporate the significance of early readiness, the requirement for fair admittance to assets, and the acknowledgment of shared weaknesses despite worldwide difficulties.

Challenges envelop issues of international pressures affecting cooperative endeavors, the lopsided appropriation of assets, and worries about the viability of existing global systems. The basic to address foundational disparities, both inside and among countries, turned into a point of convergence in conversations on the post-pandemic world.

The job of authority in cultivating global joint effort became clear, stressing the requirement for conciliatory commitment, straightforward correspondence, and a promise to shared objectives. Challenges in offsetting public interests with aggregate prosperity highlighted the intricacy of exploring worldwide emergencies and the significance of comprehensive dynamic cycles.

7. **International Contemplations and Future Situations:**

International contemplations affected the elements of cooperative endeavors, with cases of collaboration and rivalry molding the worldwide reaction to the pandemic. Future situations imagine an existence where the illustrations gained from the pandemic illuminate a more cooperative, tough, and comprehensive global request.

The investigation of cooperative endeavors among countries and worldwide establishments brought up issues about the job of international contemplations in affecting the direction of global participation. Finding some kind of harmony between public interests and aggregate prosperity arose as a basic test, requiring discretionary expertise, successful multilateralism, and a promise to shared values.

Future situations imagine an existence where the cooperative soul that arose during the pandemic continues, impacting worldwide administration structures, financial practices, and emergency reaction systems. The job of worldwide establishments in cultivating participation, the significance of political commitment to settling clashes, and the basic of tending to foundational disparities are focal subjects in forming an additional cooperative and economical future.

3.2 Examination of global initiatives aimed at economic recovery

The assessment of worldwide drives focused on monetary recuperation in the result of the Coronavirus pandemic uncovers a perplexing scene of difficulties, reactions, and systems utilized by countries and global associations. This extensive examination digs into the different elements of monetary recuperation endeavors, going from financial arrangements to feasible improvement drives and the job of mechanical headways.

1. **Financial Improvement and Money related Strategies:**
   Following the pandemic, states overall executed phenomenal monetary improvement measures to balance the financial slump. Enormous scope spending programs, tax reductions, and monetary guide to organizations and people were conveyed to help interest and forestall a delayed downturn. National banks, in a joint effort with financial specialists, executed money related strategies, for example, bringing down loan fees and giving liquidity backing to settle monetary business sectors.

   The viability of these drives fluctuated across nations, contingent upon their financial limit, strategy structures, and the seriousness of the monetary effect. While cutting edge economies had more noteworthy financial space to execute sweeping upgrade bundles, emerging countries confronted difficulties because of restricted assets and elevated degrees of obligation. The assessment of financial and money related strategies highlights the significance of a planned and fitted way to deal with address the different monetary conditions of countries.

2. **Practical Advancement Objectives (SDGs) and Comprehensive Recuperation:**
   Worldwide drives focused on monetary recuperation progressively stress the mix of supportable improvement standards. The Unified Countries' Practical Improvement Objectives (SDGs) act as a directing structure for recuperation endeavors, stressing the need to address social, financial, and ecological difficulties at the same time. Policymakers and worldwide associations perceive that cultivating comprehensive and practical advancement is fundamental for building flexibility against future emergencies.

   Endeavors to adjust recuperation plans with the SDGs include putting resources into environmentally friendly power, advancing comprehensive development, and tending to disparities. Green recuperation drives, which focus on natural maintainability, got some decent forward movement as countries tried to all the while resuscitate economies and address environmental change. The assessment of such drives features the acknowledgment that monetary recuperation ought to be sought after in a manner that advances long haul manageability and versatility.

3. **Computerized Change and Mechanical Development:**
   The pandemic sped up the reception of computerized advances, reshaping the financial scene and affecting recuperation procedures. Computerized change drives became integral to financial recuperation, with an emphasis on upgrading efficiency, further developing network, and encouraging advancement. Remote work, online business, and advanced administrations assumed urgent parts in keeping up with financial exercises during lockdowns.

Worldwide drives pointed toward utilizing innovation for recuperation remember ventures for advanced foundation, support for innovation new companies, and the improvement of computerized proficiency programs. The assessment of these drives uncovers the potential for innovation to drive financial development, yet it likewise highlights the significance of addressing computerized partitions to guarantee evenhanded access and incorporation.

4. **Global Exchange and Monetary Reconciliation:**

   Worldwide drives in monetary recuperation include rejuvenating global exchange and financial reconciliation. While the pandemic at first prompted disturbances in worldwide stockpile chains and an ascent in protectionist gauges, the basic of monetary recuperation provoked endeavors to work with exchange and eliminate boundaries. Global associations like the World Exchange Association (WTO) assumed parts in organizing exchange arrangements and forestalling the acceleration of exchange strains.

   The assessment of worldwide exchange drives uncovers a sensitive harmony between public interests and the acknowledgment of the advantages of a universally interconnected economy. Endeavors to reinforce worldwide collaboration in exchange include tending to exchange lopsided characteristics, lessening duties, and encouraging a more open and unsurprising exchanging framework.

5. **Foundation Venture and Occupation Creation:**

   To invigorate financial recuperation, numerous countries left on foundation venture projects pointed toward making position and helping monetary action. Huge scope interests in areas like transportation, energy, and medical care add to both prompt work creation and long haul financial development. Global associations, perceiving the multiplier impact of framework spending, have pushed for facilitated endeavors to speed up such tasks.

   The assessment of foundation venture drives uncovers the potential for work creation, further developed efficiency, and upgraded seriousness. In any case, challenges incorporate funding limitations, project execution delays, and the need to guarantee that foundation projects line up with supportability objectives.

6. **Social Security Nets and Comprehensive Arrangements:**

   The financial effect of the pandemic lopsidedly impacted weak populaces, inciting the execution of social wellbeing nets and comprehensive approaches. Numerous nations presented or extended social assurance programs, offering monetary help to people and organizations most impacted by the emergency. Worldwide associations, perceiving the significance of social security nets in advancing comprehensive recuperation, have upheld for proceeded with help and extension of such projects.

   The assessment of social security net drives underlines the job of designated and very much planned approaches in alleviating the social and financial effect of the pandemic. Guaranteeing the inclusivity of recuperation endeavors includes tending to disparities, supporting minimized networks, and planning arrangements that focus on the most helpless.

7. **Obligation Alleviation and Monetary Help:**
Non-industrial countries confronted huge difficulties in overseeing elevated degrees of obligation exacerbated by the financial effect of the pandemic. Worldwide drives focused on monetary recuperation incorporate obligation help programs and monetary help to nations battling with obligation loads. Global monetary organizations, like the Worldwide Money related Asset (IMF) and the World Bank, play played parts in offering monetary help and upholding for obligation rebuilding.

The assessment of obligation help drives highlights the requirement for a planned and complete way to deal with address the obligation challenges looked by non-industrial countries. The significance of fair and manageable obligation rehearses is featured as countries team up to forestall an extended obligation emergency that could block worldwide monetary recuperation.

8. **Illustrations Learned and Progressing Difficulties:**
The assessment of worldwide drives focused on financial recuperation gives significant examples to future emergency the board and recuperation arranging. One key example is the significance of worldwide cooperation and coordination in tending to a worldwide emergency. The pandemic uncovered the interconnectedness of economies and the requirement for an aggregate reaction to challenges that rise above public lines.

Continuous difficulties incorporate the lopsided dissemination of immunizations, industrious international pressures, and the need to address fundamental disparities. The assessment of these difficulties highlights the intricacy of exploring a post-pandemic world and the basic of supported global collaboration.

9. **International Contemplations and Future Situations:**

International contemplations have impacted the elements of worldwide monetary recuperation drives. Pressures between significant powers, exchange questions, and contending public interests have formed the international scene. Future situations imagine a reality where international contemplations keep on assuming a critical part in financial recuperation endeavors.

The assessment of international contemplations highlights the requirement for tact, discourse, and worldwide collaboration to explore complex international difficulties. Future situations include situations where countries figure out something worth agreeing on, conquer contrasts, and team up to address shared difficulties.

Be that as it may, difficulties like protectionism, patriotism, and international competitions might keep on presenting obstacles to consistent worldwide monetary recuperation.

3.3 Challenges and opportunities in fostering international solidarity

Encouraging worldwide fortitude, particularly even with worldwide difficulties, for example, the Coronavirus pandemic, presents a complicated scene set apart by both critical difficulties and promising open doors. This exhaustive investigation dives into the complex parts of advancing global fortitude, looking at the obstacles that block participation and the expected open doors for building an additional interconnected and cooperative world.

Challenges in Cultivating Worldwide Fortitude:

International Strains:

One of the essential difficulties to global fortitude stems from international pressures among countries. Contending public interests, authentic struggles, and power elements can thwart aggregate activity. During the pandemic, international contemplations impacted the dispersion of assets, immunization access, and worldwide reaction endeavors, featuring the fragile equilibrium expected to beat political contrasts and encourage certified fortitude.

Financial Disparities:

Monetary incongruities both inside and among countries present critical boundaries to fortitude. The pandemic exacerbated existing imbalances, with weak populaces and emerging countries confronting unbalanced difficulties. Admittance to antibodies, medical services assets, and financial recuperation measures became challenged issues, highlighting the requirement for addressing primary monetary disparities to advance genuine worldwide fortitude.

Patriotism and Protectionism:

The ascent of patriotism and protectionist opinions in certain districts hampers the soul of coordinated effort. The quest for public interests over aggregate prosperity can prompt the storing of assets, inconsistent dissemination of advantages, and a hesitance to take part in worldwide collaboration. Conquering these propensities requires a change in mentality towards perceiving shared difficulties that rise above borders.

General Wellbeing Difficulties:

In spite of the worldwide idea of general wellbeing emergencies like the pandemic, challenges continue organizing powerful reactions.

Issues, for example, inconsistent admittance to medical care, immunization conveyance leaps, and changing degrees of readiness among countries feature the intricacies of accomplishing a brought together worldwide wellbeing procedure. Reinforcing worldwide wellbeing administration and collaboration is fundamental for tending to future wellbeing crises.

Environmental Change and Natural Stewardship:

The natural difficulties presented by environmental change highlight the need for worldwide fortitude. Be that as it may, varying needs, monetary interests, and the battle for asset distribution can block aggregate activity. Overcoming any issues among created and emerging countries, alongside tending to the main drivers of natural corruption, stays an impressive test.

Data Sharing and Falsehood:

Successful worldwide fortitude depends on straightforward data sharing and an aggregate comprehension of worldwide difficulties. Be that as it may, deception and the particular sharing of data can sabotage trust and obstruct composed endeavors. Reinforcing correspondence channels, fighting falsehood, and advancing a culture of shared information are essential for cultivating global fortitude.

Philanthropic Emergencies and Struggle:

Progressing compassionate emergencies and equipped contentions upset endeavors to fabricate fortitude. Dislodged populaces, stressed assets, and international contentions add to the intricacy of global collaboration. Settling clashes and tending to the main drivers of philanthropic emergencies are fundamental stages towards establishing a climate helpful for fortitude.

Potential open doors for Cultivating Global Fortitude:

Worldwide Wellbeing Collaboration:

The experience of the pandemic has highlighted the requirement for reinforced worldwide wellbeing collaboration. Potential open doors lie in supporting global foundations like the World Wellbeing Association (WHO), upgrading early admonition frameworks, and laying out components for impartial immunization dissemination. Cooperative endeavors in exploration, improvement, and creation of clinical assets can make an establishment for a more brought together reaction to future wellbeing emergencies.

Financial Flexibility and Comprehensive Development:

The quest for financial recuperation presents a valuable chance to fabricate a stronger and comprehensive worldwide economy. Cooperative drives, for example, obligation help, fair exchange rehearses, and supportable advancement objectives can address monetary imbalances.

Open doors likewise exist in encouraging development, computerized consideration, and occupation creation to guarantee that the advantages of financial recuperation are shared around the world.

Environment Activity and Supportability:

The worldwide obligation to tending to environmental change gives an extraordinary open door to global fortitude. Amazing open doors lie in executing and improving peaceful accords, putting resources into green advancements, and supporting emerging countries in their progress to feasible practices. Shared liability regarding ecological stewardship can fortify the obligations of fortitude among countries.

Innovative Coordinated effort:

The fast progression of innovation offers roads for upgraded global joint effort. Valuable open doors exist in sharing mechanical mastery, advancing computerized proficiency, and tending to the computerized partition. Cooperative endeavors in innovative work, particularly in regions like medical services innovation and sustainable power, can add to shared worldwide advancement.

Emergency Readiness and Flexibility:

The difficulties presented by the pandemic highlight the significance of proactive emergency readiness and flexibility. Open doors lie in laying out global structures for pandemic reaction, sharing prescribed procedures in emergency the board, and making stores of fundamental assets. Building an aggregate comprehension of the interconnectedness of worldwide difficulties can prepare for additional successful reactions to future emergencies.

Social Trade and Training:

Social trade and training give amazing chances to connect holes and cultivate common comprehension among countries. Drives, for example, understudy trades, social projects, and cooperative examination ventures can separate generalizations and advance a feeling of shared mankind. Building individuals to-individuals associations adds to the underpinning of worldwide fortitude.

Strategy and Compromise:

Conciliatory endeavors and compromise components assume a vital part in encouraging worldwide fortitude. Amazing open doors lie in strategic discourse, intervention cycles, and worldwide participation in settling clashes. Tending to the underlying drivers of international strains can establish a climate helpful for cooperative endeavors.

Worldwide Administration Change:

Transforming worldwide administration structures presents an amazing chance to address foundational challenges. Open doors exist in returning to and upgrading worldwide establishments to reflect contemporary real factors. A more comprehensive and delegate worldwide administration structure can work with aggregate independent direction and cultivate a feeling of shared liability.

Chapter 4

Innovations in Technology and Digital Transformation

Developments in innovation and advanced change have become characterizing powers in molding the contemporary scene across different areas. This broad investigation dives into the complex parts of mechanical headways, looking at the significant effect of developments on ventures, economies, and cultural designs.

1. **Computerized Change Across Enterprises:**
   The coming of computerized advances has introduced a change in perspective across ventures, reshaping conventional plans of action and functional structures. From money to medical services, schooling to assembling, associations are going through advanced change to remain serious in the quickly developing scene. Distributed computing, man-made brainpower (simulated intelligence), the Web of Things (IoT), and blockchain are among the key innovations driving this groundbreaking wave.
   In finance, digitalization has led to fintech, reforming installment frameworks, web based banking, and the development of cryptographic forms of money. In medical services, telemedicine, wellbeing data frameworks, and wearable gadgets are changing patient consideration and information the board. The training area is seeing the multiplication of e-learning stages, virtual homerooms, and customized opportunities for growth. In the interim, savvy fabricating, empowered by advancements like IoT and computerization, is upgrading creation cycles and store network the executives.

2. **Man-made brainpower and AI:**
   Man-made brainpower (simulated intelligence) and AI (ML) address a mechanical outskirts with significant ramifications for different fields. Artificial intelligence calculations, equipped for gaining from information and pursuing astute choices, are being bridled in assorted applications. In medical care, man-made intelligence supports diagnostics, drug revelation, and customized therapy plans. In finance, it powers misrepresentation identification frameworks, algorithmic

exchanging, and credit scoring. Computer based intelligence driven chatbots and menial helpers are improving client assistance across enterprises.

AI calculations, a subset of computer based intelligence, empower frameworks to learn examples and make forecasts without express programming. This innovation underlies proposal motors on stages like Netflix and Amazon, customized promoting systems, and prescient support in assembling. Notwithstanding, moral contemplations, straightforwardness, and predisposition in artificial intelligence calculations present difficulties that require cautious route as these innovations keep on progressing.

3. **Blockchain Innovation:**

Blockchain, initially intended to support digital forms of money like Bitcoin, has developed into a troublesome innovation with applications past the monetary area. A decentralized and secure record framework, blockchain guarantees straightforwardness, recognizability, and carefully designed record-keeping. In finance, blockchain is upsetting exchanges, working with quicker and safer cross-line installments. Production network the executives benefits from blockchain's capacity to give an unchanging record of each and every exchange, improving responsibility and diminishing misrepresentation.

Also, blockchain is changing the idea of shrewd agreements, self-executing concurrences with the terms straightforwardly composed into code. These agreements smooth out processes, robotize consistence, and diminish the requirement for mediators. Regardless of its true capacity, challenges connected with versatility, administrative systems, and normalization need addressing for blockchain to arrive at its maximum capacity.

4. **The Web of Things (IoT):**

The Web of Things (IoT) includes an organization of interconnected gadgets installed with sensors, programming, and network, empowering them to gather and trade information. In the time of shrewd homes, wearable gadgets, and modern IoT, the ramifications of this innovation are immense. In medical care, IoT gadgets screen patients' important bodily functions and send information to medical services suppliers progressively, empowering far off quiet observing and proactive medical care mediations.

In the modern area, IoT adds to the idea of Industry 4.0, where savvy manufacturing plants influence interconnected gadgets for effective creation, prescient upkeep, and constant observing. Brilliant urban areas use IoT for traffic the board, squander decrease, and energy streamlining. Notwithstanding, worries about information security, protection, and the interoperability of different IoT biological systems require consideration as the sending of these advances keeps on developing.

5. **Online protection Difficulties:**

The multiplication of advanced innovations additionally delivers online protection challenges as associations wrestle with the need to get huge measures of delicate information. Cyberattacks, going from ransomware to information breaks, present critical dangers to people, organizations, and state run administrations. The rising complexity of digital dangers requires nonstop development in online protection measures.

Man-made consciousness is assuming a pivotal part in network protection, empowering the fast discovery of irregularities and the forecast of possible dangers. Blockchain innovation is likewise being investigated to upgrade the security of information stockpiling and exchanges. As associations embrace a proactive way to deal with online protection, joint effort, data sharing, and the improvement of strong security systems become principal in defending computerized environments.

6. **Computerized Consideration and Availability:**

While mechanical developments offer remarkable open doors, worries about advanced incorporation and availability endure. The advanced gap, portrayed by abberations in admittance to innovation, web availability, and computerized education, compounds social and financial imbalances. Overcoming this issue is fundamental to guarantee that the advantages of mechanical headways are open to all.

Endeavors to improve computerized consideration include drives to give reasonable web access, advance computerized education programs, and foster innovations with an emphasis on openness. The fair sending of innovation adds to a more comprehensive society, where people of different foundations have the potential chance to take part completely in the computerized economy.

7. **Increased and Computer generated Reality:**

Increased reality (AR) and augmented reality (VR) are vivid advances that have tracked down applications across different areas, changing the manner in which individuals communicate with the computerized world. AR overlays advanced data onto the actual climate, upgrading certifiable encounters. VR, then again, establishes a reenacted climate, drenching clients in a PC produced reality.

In schooling, AR and VR offer vivid opportunities for growth, empowering understudies to investigate verifiable destinations, direct virtual tests, and draw in with complex ideas. In medical services, specialists use AR for careful route, and VR is utilized for helpful mediations, like openness treatment for fears. As these innovations advance, addressing difficulties connected with equipment costs, content turn of events, and potential cultural effects becomes pivotal for their inescapable reception.

8. **5G Innovation:**

The rollout of 5G innovation addresses a huge jump forward in network, promising quicker information speeds, lower dormancy, and expanded network limit. Past empowering quicker web perusing on cell phones, 5G holds groundbreaking potential for different areas. In medical services, the low dormancy of 5G works with ongoing far off medical procedures and telemedicine applications.

In assembling, it upholds the organization of brilliant processing plants with improved computerization and correspondence capacities.

Notwithstanding, the broad organization of 5G additionally raises worries about potential wellbeing chances, security weaknesses, and the requirement for powerful administrative systems. Finding some kind of harmony between the advantages of upgraded availability and tending to these worries is significant for the effective combination of 5G innovation.

9. **Moral Contemplations in Mechanical Progressions:**

As innovation keeps on progressing, moral contemplations become foremost in guaranteeing that advancements benefit humankind without actually hurting. Computer based intelligence, specifically, raises moral worries connected with pre-disposition in calculations, attack of security, and the possible abuse of independent frameworks. Finding some kind of harmony among development and moral standards requires proactive endeavors in creating moral structures, laying out industry principles, and cultivating a culture of mindful advancement.

Notwithstanding simulated intelligence, different advances like biotechnology, hereditary designing, and neurotechnology additionally raise moral situations that request cautious thought. Moral conversations ought to include different partners, including technologists, policymakers, ethicists, and the more extensive public to guarantee a thorough and comprehensive way to deal with moral dynamic in the domain of mechanical progressions.

4.1 Impact of technological advancements on economic recovery

The effect of mechanical headways on financial recuperation is a diverse and dynamic peculiarity that has acquired noticeable quality, especially directly following worldwide difficulties like the Coronavirus pandemic. This investigation dives into the different elements of how innovation shapes financial recuperation endeavors, looking at the groundbreaking job it plays across businesses and the more extensive ramifications for social orders and economies.

1. **Computerized Change as an Impetus for Monetary Strength:**

   The Coronavirus pandemic went about as an impetus for sped up computer-ized change, inciting organizations and states to reevaluate their methodologies and embrace imaginative innovations. Digitalization turned into a key part for monetary strength, permitting associations to adjust quickly to interruptions and proceed with tasks in the midst of lockdowns and limitations. The capacity to lead business from a distance, influence web based business, and execute computerized answers for different cycles became basic parts of monetary re-cuperation.

   The coordination of distributed computing, man-made brainpower, and in-formation examination enabled organizations to upgrade activities, improve effectiveness, and go with informed choices progressively. From private companies to enormous ventures, the reception of computerized devices became an upper hand as well as an endurance basic during testing times.

2. **Remote Work and the Change of the Labor force:**
One of the main effects of mechanical headways on financial recuperation has been the broad reception of remote work. As organizations went to computerized cooperation devices, video conferencing stages, and cloud-based project the executives frameworks, the conventional office arrangement went through a change in outlook. This shift permitted associations to support their tasks as well as introduced open doors for rethinking the fate of work.

   Remote work worked with geographic adaptability, empowering organizations to take advantage of a worldwide ability pool. This, thus, added to expanded labor force variety and inclusivity. In any case, challenges connected with keeping up with representative commitment, guaranteeing evenhanded admittance to potential open doors, and addressing the computerized partition as far as admittance to innovation and a helpful remote workplace arose, highlighting the requirement for all encompassing ways to deal with labor force change.

3. **Online business and the Rehash of Retail:**
The speed increase of web based business has been a characterizing component of the mechanical effect on financial recuperation. With lockdowns and social separating estimates set up, customers progressively went to online stages for their shopping needs.

   Retailers that had put resources into hearty web based business foundations endured the hardship as well as frequently experienced development during the pandemic.

   The digitalization of retail activities, from online exchanges to production network the executives, stressed the significance of spryness and flexibility. Man-made consciousness driven customized proposals, virtual take a stab at encounters, and contactless installment frameworks became necessary to the internet business scene. Notwithstanding, difficulties, for example, network protection dangers, information security concerns, and the requirement for improved advanced proficiency warrant progressing consideration as web based business keeps on molding the retail scene.

4. **Monetary Innovation (Fintech) and Comprehensive Money:**
Mechanical headways have likewise fundamentally affected the monetary area, with the ascent of fintech assuming a significant part in financial recuperation. Fintech developments include an expansive range, from computerized installment arrangements and blockchain-based monetary administrations to robo-consultants and distributed loaning stages. These developments have democratized admittance to monetary administrations, advancing monetary consideration and versatility even with financial vulnerabilities.

   Blockchain innovation, with its decentralized and straightforward nature, can possibly upset conventional monetary frameworks. Cryptographic forms of money and national bank computerized monetary standards (CBDCs) stand out as advanced options in contrast to conventional monetary forms. Be that as it may, administrative difficulties, worries about monetary steadiness, and the requirement for purchaser security require cautious thought in coordinating these advances into standard monetary frameworks.

5. **High level Assembling and Industry 4.0:**

The crossing point of innovation and assembling, frequently alluded to as Industry 4.0, has been instrumental in improving monetary recuperation. Shrewd assembling processes influence advancements like the Web of Things (IoT), large information investigation, and man-made reasoning to enhance creation, further develop inventory network the board, and empower prescient upkeep.

The capacity to screen and examine information progressively works with effective asset designation, decreases personal time, and improves by and large efficiency. Computerization and mechanical technology have additionally added to labor force productivity, empowering human specialists to zero in on complex errands while redundant and routine capabilities are mechanized. While these headways hold the commitment of expanded seriousness and versatility in assembling, tending to worries about work dislodging, upskilling the labor force, and guaranteeing the moral utilization of innovation stay basic.

6. **Medical care Innovation and Telemedicine:**

The medical care area has seen a significant effect from mechanical progressions, particularly with regards to the Coronavirus pandemic. Telemedicine arose as a basic device for conveying medical care benefits from a distance, guaranteeing coherence of care while limiting the gamble of infection transmission. Computerized wellbeing arrangements, including wearable gadgets and wellbeing observing applications, got some decent forward movement in checking and dealing with patients' wellbeing progressively.

Man-made consciousness in medical services has been urgent in speeding up diagnostics, drug disclosure, and immunization advancement. AI calculations dissect tremendous datasets to distinguish designs, foresee sickness flare-ups, and customize therapy plans. The joining of innovation in medical services added to pandemic reaction as well as established the groundwork for a more associated and patient-driven medical services biological system.

7. **Supportable Advances and Green Progress:**

Mechanical progressions have likewise assumed an essential part in driving supportability drives and the change to greener economies. Environmentally friendly power innovations, brilliant lattice frameworks, and energy-proficient arrangements have acquired unmistakable quality as countries endeavor to meet environment objectives. The reception of electric vehicles, combined with progressions in battery innovation, is reshaping the auto business and adding to the decrease of fossil fuel byproducts.

Shrewd urban communities influence innovation to streamline asset utilization, lessen ecological effect, and improve the personal satisfaction for inhabitants. Notwithstanding, the progress to practical advancements faces difficulties, for example, high execution costs, administrative structures, and the requirement for worldwide joint effort to altogether resolve worldwide ecological issues.

8. **Difficulties and Contemplations:**

While innovative progressions achieve extraordinary open doors, they likewise bring about difficulties that require cautious thought. The computerized partition, portrayed by variations in admittance to innovation and computerized proficiency, represents a gamble of fueling existing imbalances. Security concerns, moral contemplations, and the expected abuse of advances highlight the significance of dependable development and powerful administrative systems.

The quick speed of innovative change likewise requests a deft and versatile labor force. Upskilling and reskilling drives become fundamental to outfit people with the skills expected to flourish in a mechanically determined economy. Besides, addressing concerns connected with work dislodging and guaranteeing that the advantages of innovative progressions are shared comprehensively is necessary to encouraging a strong and evenhanded monetary recuperation.

4.2 Industries leveraging digital transformation

Computerized change has turned into an unavoidable power, reshaping the scene of different ventures across the globe. This extensive investigation digs into the significant effect of advanced change on different areas, inspecting how organizations are utilizing innovation to upgrade activities, further develop client encounters, and drive development.

1. **Money and Banking:**
   The monetary business has gone through an extreme change with the coming of computerized innovations. Conventional financial models have given way to internet banking, portable installment arrangements, and the ascent of monetary innovation (fintech) organizations. Computerized change in finance envelops a scope of developments, including blockchain for secure and straightforward exchanges, robo-counselors for mechanized speculation the executives, and versatile banking applications for consistent client encounters.
   Computerized reasoning (man-made intelligence) is utilized for misrepresentation identification, risk evaluation, and customized client administrations. AI calculations investigate tremendous datasets to give experiences into market patterns, empowering more educated navigation. Cryptographic forms of money and decentralized finance (DeFi) stages address the boondocks of computerized development in finance, testing customary ideas of cash and banking.

2. **Retail and Internet business:**

The retail area has seen a seismic shift with the ascent of internet business and computerized innovations. Web based shopping stages, customized proposals, and portable installment frameworks have become indispensable parts of the cutting edge retail insight. Retailers influence information examination to figure out shopper inclinations, enhance estimating systems, and smooth out store network activities.

Developments like expanded reality (AR) are changing the manner in which clients draw in with items, permitting virtual attempt ons and improving the general shopping experience. Man-made reasoning is utilized for request guaging, stock administration, and chatbots for client care. Advanced change in retail reaches out past the web-based domain, with shrewd advances upgrading in-store encounters through the Web of Things (IoT) gadgets and contactless installment arrangements.

3. **Medical services and Telemedicine:**

The medical services industry is going through a computerized unrest, set apart by the reception of telemedicine, electronic wellbeing records (EHRs), and high level clinical innovations. Telemedicine stages empower far off counsels, further developing admittance to medical care administrations and decreasing the weight on conventional medical care framework. Advanced wellbeing arrangements, including wearable gadgets and wellbeing observing applications, engage people to proactively deal with their wellbeing.

Man-made reasoning assumes a significant part in diagnostics, drug revelation, and treatment arranging. AI calculations examine clinical information to distinguish designs, foresee illness results, and customize treatment plans. Mechanical technology aid medical procedures, and IoT gadgets screen patients continuously, giving medical services experts complete bits of knowledge. The combination of advanced innovations improves proficiency, lessens medical services costs, and adds to more persistent driven care models.

4. **Assembling and Industry 4.0:**

The assembling area is going through an extraordinary cycle known as Industry 4.0, described by the coordination of computerized innovations into assembling processes. Shrewd processing plants influence IoT gadgets, information investigation, and robotization to upgrade creation, further develop proficiency, and empower prescient upkeep. High level mechanical technology and AI add to the development of shrewd assembling frameworks.

Advanced twin innovation makes virtual imitations of actual resources, permitting producers to mimic and dissect different situations prior to executing changes. Inventory network the board benefits from ongoing information investigation, improving perceivability and responsiveness. The consistent mix of innovation in assembling further develops efficiency as well as works with a more deft and versatile industry.

5. **Schooling and E-Learning:**

The schooling area has encountered a critical change with the coming of computerized innovations. E-learning stages, virtual homerooms, and online cooperation instruments have become fundamental parts of present day instruction. Computerized content conveyance, intelligent opportunities for growth, and gamification procedures are reshaping conventional instructing techniques.

Man-made consciousness is used for customized learning, versatile evaluations, and wise coaching frameworks. Information examination give experiences into understudy execution, assisting teachers with fitting educational methodologies. Expanded reality upgrades instructive encounters, permitting understudies to associate with programmatic experiences and three-layered models. The digitalization of training extends admittance to learning assets as well as cultivates a more adaptable and customized learning climate.

6. **Media communications and 5G Innovation:**

   The media communications industry is at the bleeding edge of advanced change, with the approach of 5G innovation promising phenomenal availability. 5G organizations give quicker information speeds, lower dormancy, and expanded limit, empowering the consistent joining of arising innovations like the Web of Things (IoT) and increased reality.

   The arrangement of 5G is ready to reform different areas, from medical care and assembling to brilliant urban communities and independent vehicles. Improved availability works with continuous correspondence, upholds the expansion of IoT gadgets, and empowers the advancement of imaginative applications. The media communications industry, through computerized change, turns into a key empowering influence of network and innovative headways across different spaces.

7. **Energy and Shrewd Frameworks:**

   The energy area is utilizing advanced change to improve effectiveness, supportability, and strength. Brilliant frameworks, empowered by IoT gadgets and information investigation, streamline energy dispersion, decrease wastage, and upgrade lattice unwavering quality. Progressed metering framework permits buyers to screen and deal with their energy utilization progressively.

   Environmentally friendly power innovations, for example, sunlight based and wind, are incorporated with advanced answers for enhance power age and capacity. AI calculations anticipate energy request designs, empowering better asset allotment and lattice the executives. Advanced innovations add to the change toward more maintainable and decentralized energy frameworks, diminishing dependence on conventional petroleum derivatives.

8. **Transportation and Independent Vehicles:**

   The transportation business is going through an upheaval with the coming of computerized innovations, especially in the improvement of independent vehicles. Associated vehicles, furnished with sensors and correspondence advancements, upgrade security and empower continuous traffic the executives. The reconciliation of man-made brainpower empowers vehicles to settle on information driven choices, explore complex conditions, and speak with one another.

The ascent of ride-sharing stages, empowered by versatile applications and geolocation administrations, changes the manner in which individuals access transportation administrations. Electric vehicles, combined with progressions in battery innovation, add to a more feasible and harmless to the ecosystem transportation biological system. Advanced change in transportation stretches out past individual vehicles to envelop brilliant urban communities' drives, advancing productive and eco-accommodating metropolitan portability arrangements.

9. **Media and Amusement:**

The media and media outlet has gone through a significant computerized change, driven by the expansion of internet real time features, web-based entertainment stages, and advanced content creation.

Streaming stages follow through on-request satisfied to worldwide crowds, testing conventional telecom models. Web-based entertainment stages have become fundamental to content conveyance, crowd commitment, and showcasing procedures.

Man-made reasoning is utilized for content proposal calculations, customized client encounters, and, surprisingly, in the making of computerized content. Virtual and expanded reality advancements upgrade vivid encounters in gaming and amusement. Computerized change has democratized content creation, permitting people to deliver and disperse content universally, testing conventional gatekeeping structures.

4.3 Prospects for sustained growth through technological innovation

The possibilities for supported development through mechanical advancement are necessary to the development of economies, businesses, and social orders. This extensive investigation digs into the multi-layered elements of how mechanical development fills in as an impetus for supported monetary development, encouraging headways in different areas, driving efficiency, and molding the fate of worldwide advancement.

1. **Development as a Driver of Financial Development:**
   Mechanical development remains at the very front of driving financial development by cultivating inventiveness, productivity, and seriousness. Through the consistent turn of events and use of new advances, enterprises become more useful, productive, and strong. Development is a vital figure making esteem, opening new business sectors, and giving answers for arising difficulties. Countries that focus on and put resources into advancement make the circumstances for supported monetary development, as proven by authentic and contemporary models.
   The appearance of weighty advances, for example, the steam motor during the Modern Unrest or the ascent of the web in the late twentieth hundred years, represents how development can change economies. In the contemporary

scene, arising advancements like man-made reasoning, biotechnology, and environmentally friendly power hold the commitment of molding another time of supported development.

2. **Innovation and Efficiency Gains:**

   Mechanical development contributes essentially to efficiency gains, a basic figure supported monetary development. Mechanization, man-made brainpower, and high level assembling processes smooth out activities, diminish expenses, and improve proficiency across different ventures. The expanded productivity of creation processes not just permits organizations to deliver more with less assets yet additionally cultivates the advancement of altogether new items and administrations.

   As organizations influence innovation to further develop their creation capacities, the general result of economies encounters a vertical direction. The idea of "imaginative obliteration," presented by financial analyst Joseph Schumpeter, underscores how advancement upsets existing ventures and plans of action at the end of the day prompts higher by and large efficiency and monetary development.

3. **Business and New companies:**

   Mechanical development gives prolific ground to business venture and the development of new companies, adding to work creation, market dynamism, and financial strength. In a time where troublesome advances can quickly change ventures, new companies are frequently at the very front of presenting novel arrangements and testing laid out standards. State run administrations and establishments that encourage a climate helpful for advancement, with steady approaches, admittance to financing, and foundation, engage business visionaries to drive supported monetary development.

   The examples of overcoming adversity of tech goliaths that started as new businesses, like Google, Facebook, and Amazon, highlight the extraordinary force of pioneering advancement. These organizations made new business sectors as well as reshaped whole enterprises, exhibiting the potential for supported monetary development through the problematic power of mechanical business.

4. **Globalization and Availability:**

   Mechanical development assumes a crucial part in encouraging globalization and upgrading worldwide network. The computerized upset, embodied by the web and high level correspondence innovations, has changed the manner in which organizations work on a worldwide scale. Admittance to data, consistent correspondence, and the capacity to direct business across borders add to the development of business sectors, exchange, and financial interconnectedness.

   Worldwide stockpile chains, empowered by mechanical headways in strategies and correspondence, consider more proficient creation cycles and asset designation. Developments in monetary innovations work with cross-line exchanges and speculation, encouraging a more interconnected and dynamic worldwide economy. The ceaseless development of availability through innovation upgrades open doors for worldwide cooperation and exchange, advancing supported financial development.

5. **Interest in Innovative work:**

A pivotal driver of mechanical advancement is interest in innovative work (Research and development). Countries and enterprises that assign assets to logical examination, mechanical turn of events, and advancement biological systems are better situated for supported development.

States, confidential undertakings, and instructive establishments that focus on Research and development establish a climate where advancement revelations and innovative headways can prosper.

All things considered, times of huge mechanical advancement have been related with expanded Research and development speculation. For instance, the space race during the twentieth century prompted progressions in registering and materials science. Today, interests in regions like biotechnology, man-made consciousness, and green advancements hold the possibility to catalyze extraordinary changes with extensive ramifications for supported financial development.

6. **Arising Advancements and Industry 4.0:**

The Fourth Modern Unrest, frequently alluded to as Industry 4.0, is portrayed by the combination of arising innovations like man-made consciousness, the Web of Things (IoT), advanced mechanics, and huge information investigation into modern cycles. This combination of advances can possibly reclassify whole enterprises, encouraging expanded effectiveness, customization, and manageability.

In assembling, Industry 4.0 addresses a shift toward savvy processing plants where interconnected machines convey and upgrade creation continuously. In medical services, the utilization of information examination and artificial intelligence adds to customized medication and worked on understanding results. The reception of these advances across different areas holds the commitment of upgrading efficiency as well as making new plans of action and markets, driving supported monetary development.

7. **Environmentally friendly power and Supportable Advancement:**

Mechanical development is a critical driver in the progress toward a more reasonable and harmless to the ecosystem economy. The improvement of sustainable power advancements, for example, sun based and wind power, addresses a change in perspective in the energy area. Maintainable advancement tends to ecological difficulties as well as sets out new monetary open doors and occupations in arising businesses.

Interests in clean energy advancements add to diminishing reliance on petroleum products, alleviating environmental change, and advancing energy autonomy. Legislatures and organizations that embrace economical development not just position themselves as pioneers in a developing business sector yet additionally add to a stronger and environmentally adjusted worldwide economy.

8. Difficulties and Contemplations:

While the possibilities for supported development through mechanical advancement are colossal, certain difficulties and contemplations should be tended to. Moral worries encompassing the utilization of arising innovations, information protection issues, and the potential for work relocation because of computerization require smart thought. Moreover, the advanced gap, portrayed by variations in admittance to innovation, should be addressed to guarantee that the advantages of development are comprehensive and open to all.

The speed of innovative change likewise requires an emphasis on schooling and abilities improvement. The labor force representing things to come should be furnished with the abilities expected to explore a quickly developing innovative scene. Long lasting picking up, upskilling, and reskilling drives are significant parts of encouraging a labor force that can add to and benefit from supported mechanical development.

Chapter 5

Sustainable Development and Green Initiatives

Practical turn of events and green drives address a change in outlook in how social orders approach financial development, natural preservation, and social prosperity. This extensive investigation digs into the complex components of maintainable turn of events, looking at the rules that support it, the difficulties looked in its execution, and the groundbreaking capability of green drives in forming a stronger and fair future.

1. **Standards of Practical Turn of events:**
   Practical improvement is an all encompassing and ground breaking approach that looks to address the issues of the present without compromising the capacity of people in the future to address their own issues. At its center, supportable improvement coordinates financial, social, and ecological contemplations to make a fair and strong system for development. The standards of reasonable turn of events, as expressed in milestone archives like the Brundtland Report, stress the interconnectedness of financial advancement, social value, and natural stewardship.

   Financial manageability includes encouraging comprehensive development that helps all sections of society while advancing productive asset usage. Social supportability means to guarantee social value, equity, and prosperity, enveloping angles like schooling, medical services, and local area improvement. Ecological manageability underlines the dependable administration of regular assets, decrease of natural effect, and the advancement of biodiversity and environment wellbeing.

2. **Environmentally friendly power and Progress to a Low-Carbon Economy:**
   Key to practical improvement is the progress to environmentally friendly power sources and the quest for a low-carbon economy. The dependence on petroleum derivatives for energy has for some time been a driver of ecological corruption and environmental change. Green drives as sun powered, wind, hydro, and geothermal energy offer cleaner and more feasible other options, diminishing ozone

harming substance outflows and alleviating environment related gambles.

Nations and organizations embracing sustainable power add to natural preservation as well as position themselves as pioneers in a worldwide shift toward maintainability. The improvement of brilliant networks, energy capacity arrangements, and energy-productive advancements further upgrades the suitability and adaptability of sustainable power drives. As the world endeavors to accomplish the objectives set in the Paris Understanding, the reception of environmentally friendly power turns into a key part in reasonable improvement endeavors.

3. **Roundabout Economy and Asset Productivity:**

The idea of a roundabout economy is indispensable to supportable turn of events, stressing the decrease of waste, the reuse of materials, and the reusing of assets. Conventional direct monetary models, portrayed by a "take, make, arrange" approach, are being supplanted by roundabout models that focus on asset effectiveness and limit ecological effect.

Green drives advancing a round economy include overhauling items for life span, encouraging reusing foundation, and boosting dependable utilization. By decoupling monetary development from asset utilization, a round economy adds to the preservation of limited assets, lessens contamination, and sets out financial open doors through the improvement of reasonable inventory chains.

4. **Biodiversity Protection and Biological system Reclamation:**

Defending biodiversity and reestablishing biological systems are key parts of feasible turn of events. Biodiversity, including the assortment of life on The planet, gives fundamental environment administrations like fertilization, water sanitization, and environment guideline. Green drives focused on biodiversity preservation include the assurance of normal living spaces, the foundation of safeguarded regions, and reasonable land the executives rehearses.

Biological system reclamation endeavors try to restore corrupted scenes, rejuvenate environments, and improve their strength. Reforestation projects, wetland rebuilding, and manageable horticulture rehearses add to the conservation of biodiversity and the recovery of biological systems. Perceiving the inborn worth of biodiversity and environments, maintainable improvement tries to find some kind of harmony between human turn of events and the conservation of the regular world.

5. **Green Foundation and Reasonable Urbanization:**

The course of urbanization presents the two difficulties and open doors for reasonable turn of events. Green drives in metropolitan regions center around making green foundation that upgrades the personal satisfaction for occupants while limiting natural effect. Practical urbanization includes the improvement of energy-effective structures, green spaces, and proficient public transportation frameworks.

Green rooftops, porous asphalts, and metropolitan woods add to environment versatility, diminish heat island impacts, and further develop air quality in urban areas. Savvy city drives influence innovation to advance asset use, upgrade portability, and work on in general metropolitan maintainability. By incorporating green foundation into metropolitan preparation, urban communities can become center points of development and models for reasonable living.

6. **Water Protection and Feasible Horticulture:**
Water shortage is a squeezing worldwide test that meets with maintainable improvement objectives. Green drives in water preservation envelop productive water the board rehearses, the assurance of watersheds, and the improvement of water-effective advancements. Feasible horticulture, a critical mainstay of green drives, advances rehearses that enhance crop yields while limiting ecological effect.

Accuracy agribusiness, dribble water system, and agroecological approaches add to water protection in cultivating. Reasonable agribusiness stresses soil well-being, biodiversity, and decreased dependence on compound data sources. By focusing on maintainable water use in horticulture, social orders can improve food security, safeguard biological systems, and advance the drawn out strength of water assets.

7. **Social Value and Comprehensive Turn of events:**
Reasonable improvement puts areas of strength for an on friendly value, perceiving that financial and ecological advancement should help all sections of society. Comprehensive green drives focus on minimized networks, advance social union, and address issues of neediness and imbalance. Social maintainability includes guaranteeing admittance to instruction, medical services, and monetary open doors for all.

Green positions, created through sustainable power projects, ecological protection drives, and supportable enterprises, add to comprehensive turn of events. Socially capable strategic policies, fair work practices, and local area commitment are necessary parts of green drives that try to make a more impartial and just society.

8. **Worldwide Coordinated effort and Strategy Systems:**
Manageable improvement requires worldwide cooperation and purposeful endeavors at the approach level. Peaceful accords and structures, like the Unified Countries Maintainable Improvement Objectives (SDGs) and the Paris Understanding, give a common guide to nations and partners to pursue normal supportability goals. These systems highlight the interconnectedness of worldwide difficulties and the requirement for aggregate activity.

Countries taking on aggressive focuses for discharge decrease, biodiversity protection, and neediness mitigation show a guarantee to practical turn of events. Green funding systems, advancement help, and innovation move drives support emerging nations in their quest for practical improvement objectives.

The cooperative energy of worldwide coordinated effort and vigorous approach structures establishes a climate helpful for extraordinary and enduring change.

9. **Difficulties and Contemplations:**

Regardless of the commitment and progress of maintainable turn of events and green drives, challenges endure in their far reaching reception. Monetary interests that focus on transient additions over long haul manageability, political protection from change, and the intricacies of organizing worldwide endeavors are deterrents that should be tended to. Moreover, the monetary hindrances to taking on supportable practices, particularly for non-industrial countries, present difficulties to the fair execution of green drives.

The idea of a simply progress is urgent in exploring these difficulties, guaranteeing that the shift to economical practices considers the prosperity of laborers and networks reliant upon enterprises going through change. Offsetting financial development with natural stewardship requires cautious route of compromises and the advancement of imaginative arrangements that address both prompt necessities and long haul supportability.

5.1 Importance of incorporating sustainability into economic recovery plans

The significance of integrating maintainability into financial recuperation plans has arisen as a basic thought following worldwide difficulties, especially the result of the Coronavirus pandemic.

As countries explore the way to recuperation, there is a developing acknowledgment that feasible practices are moral objectives as well as vital parts of strong and future-situated financial methodologies. This investigation digs into the diverse justifications for why maintainability should be at the center of monetary recuperation plans, enveloping ecological, social, and financial aspects.

1. **Ecological Goals and Environment Strength:**
   At the core of the push for manageability in financial recuperation lies the critical need to address ecological objectives, eminently the worldwide environment emergency. Integrating manageability into recuperation plans addresses a pledge to relieving ecological corruption, diminishing fossil fuel byproducts, and building environment strong economies. As the recurrence and power of environment related occasions increment, flexibility turns into an essential resource for countries looking to defend foundation, guarantee food and water security, and safeguard biological systems.

   Green recuperation drives, like interests in environmentally friendly power, energy-proficient foundation, and supportable transportation, add to bringing down carbon impressions and encouraging environment transformation. By focusing on environment strength in financial recuperation plans, countries line up with global environment objectives as well as future-verification their economies against the raising dangers presented by environmental change.

2. **Biodiversity Preservation and Environment Wellbeing:**
The deficiency of biodiversity and the debasement of environments are interconnected difficulties that request consideration in financial recuperation plans. Maintainability includes safeguarding and reestablishing biodiversity, perceiving the natural worth of different biological systems for environmental equilibrium, and the arrangement of fundamental administrations. Green recuperation methodologies underscore preservation endeavors, maintainable land use practices, and drives that safeguard basic territories.

Integrating supportability into financial recuperation isn't exclusively an ecological thought yet in addition an affirmation of the interconnectedness between sound biological systems and human prosperity. The protection of biodiversity guarantees the flexibility of environments, upholds farming, and adds to the general wellbeing of the planet. By incorporating these contemplations into recuperation plans, countries make ready for additional hearty and practical economies.

3. **Asset Effectiveness and Round Economy:**
The idea of a roundabout economy, portrayed by the decrease, reuse, and reusing of assets, is a foundation of manageability in financial recuperation.

Conventional straight monetary models, in light of a "take, make, arrange" approach, lead to asset exhaustion and natural contamination. Economical recuperation plans focus on asset productivity, empowering ventures to embrace round rehearses that limit squander and focus on the life span of assets.

Interests in green foundation, squander decrease drives, and maintainable creation processes add to the round economy ethos. By limiting waste and streamlining asset use, countries add to ecological protection as well as improve the productivity and seriousness of their economies. Round economy standards line up with the more extensive objective of making manageable and strong frameworks that persevere past prompt recuperation stages.

4. **Social Value and Comprehensive Development:**
Manageability in financial recuperation remains closely connected with the quest for social value and comprehensive development. The Coronavirus pandemic revealed existing social imbalances, featuring the requirement for recuperation designs that address inconsistencies and advance comprehensive financial turn of events. Practical recuperation drives focus on friendly prosperity, intending to set out open doors for all portions of society while limiting adverse consequences on weak populaces.

Interests in green positions, training, and medical services add to social supportability, encouraging versatile and engaged networks. By integrating standards of social value into recuperation plans, countries can assemble more durable and just social orders that focus on the requirements of minimized and distraught populaces. This approach lines up with moral contemplations as well as improves the general security and strength of economies.

5. **General Wellbeing and Strong Medical services Frameworks:**
The transaction between general wellbeing and maintainability has acquired noticeable quality with regards to the Coronavirus pandemic. Maintainable financial recuperation plans perceive the characteristic connection between a solid climate and human prosperity. Interests in versatile medical care frameworks, sickness avoidance, and the combination of wellbeing contemplations into metropolitan arranging add to manageable recuperation.

The pandemic highlighted the weaknesses in worldwide wellbeing frameworks and featured the significance of proactive measures for general wellbeing. Supportable recuperation plans focus on medical care framework, advanced wellbeing arrangements, and pandemic readiness. By integrating wellbeing contemplations into recuperation procedures, countries not just alleviate the effect of future wellbeing emergencies yet additionally add to the general prosperity and efficiency of their populaces.

6. **Advancement and Green Innovations:**
Manageability in monetary recuperation is inseparable from advancement and the reception of green innovations. Recuperation designs that focus on manageability outfit the extraordinary force of innovation to make more effective, versatile, and harmless to the ecosystem frameworks. Interests in sustainable power, shrewd framework, and green advances diminish natural effect as well as drive monetary development and occupation creation in arising enterprises.

Green advancement is an impetus for financial enhancement, cultivating the improvement of new business sectors and enterprises. Countries that position themselves at the front line of mechanical headways in supportability improve their worldwide seriousness as well as add to molding the ventures representing things to come. The mix of advancement into recuperation plans establishes the groundwork for reasonable financial development past quick recuperation stages.

7. **Long haul Financial Strength:**
Integrating maintainability into monetary recuperation is an essential basic for long haul financial strength. The conventional polarity between monetary development and natural preservation is progressively perceived as a bogus decision. Reasonable improvement addresses a methodology where monetary flourishing and ecological obligation are commonly building up.

Interests in green framework, environmentally friendly power, and maintainable farming add to building economies that are strong to outer shocks, whether they be monetary slumps, environment related fiascos, or general wellbeing emergencies. The expansion of economies through economical practices makes a cushion against unpredictability, situating countries for supported development despite a quickly changing worldwide scene.

8. **Worldwide Standing and Market Access:**
The worldwide shift toward maintainability has suggestions past public boundaries. Integrating manageability into monetary recuperation plans upgrades a country's worldwide standing and admittance to global business sectors. In a time where buyers, financial backers, and organizations progressively focus on moral and maintainable practices, countries that exhibit a guarantee to ecological and social obligation gain an upper hand.
Worldwide stock chains are developing to focus on supportability, and buyers are going with decisions in light of the ecological and social effect of items and administrations. Countries that position themselves as pioneers in maintainability draw in venture as well as gain market access and fabricate organizations with similar substances worldwide. This interconnectedness highlights the significance of maintainability as an essential thought in financial recuperation plans.

9. **Administrative Patterns and Future-Sealing:**
The direction of administrative patterns internationally is advancing toward additional tough ecological and social principles. Integrating supportability into monetary recuperation plans is a proactive reaction to expected administrative changes. Countries that adjust their recuperation techniques to advancing administrative assumptions consent to arising norms as well as position themselves as pioneers in capable administration.
Future-sealing economies against advancing administrative scenes includes expecting and adjusting to worldwide patterns in reasonable turn of events. By inserting manageability into recuperation plans, countries exhibit a pledge to meeting current as well as future administrative assumptions. This approach limits the dangers related with administrative rebelliousness and positions countries as dependable and capable worldwide accomplices.

10. **Local area Versatility and Partner Commitment:**

Manageability in monetary recuperation requires local area flexibility and vigorous partner commitment. Recuperation designs that include nearby networks, organizations, and common society associations make a common feeling of responsibility and responsibility. Comprehensive dynamic cycles add to the viability and acknowledgment of recuperation drives.

Local area versatility includes getting ready and enabling neighborhood populaces to endure and recuperate from different shocks, including monetary slumps, cataclysmic events, or general wellbeing crises. Feasible recuperation plans focus on friendly union, local area commitment, and the advancement of nearby limits. By encouraging local area flexibility, countries improve the versatility and responsiveness of their social orders to outer difficulties.

5.2 Countries prioritizing green initiatives

Nations focusing on green drives are at the front of a worldwide development towards maintainability, perceiving the dire need to address natural difficulties, diminish fossil fuel byproducts, and change towards stronger and eco-accommodating economies. This thorough investigation digs into the inspirations, techniques, and effect of countries that have genuinely committed to focusing on green drives in their strategy systems and improvement plans.

1. **Inspirations for Focusing on Green Drives:**

   Nations focus on green drives for various convincing reasons, driven by an acknowledgment of the interconnectedness between natural wellbeing, financial steadiness, and social prosperity. One essential inspiration is the basic to battle environmental change. Countries that focus on green drives comprehend the squeezing need to diminish ozone depleting substance emanations, progress to sustainable power sources, and construct environment versatile foundation to relieve the effects of an evolving environment.

   Another key inspiration originates from a pledge to ecological preservation and biodiversity insurance. Perceiving the important biological system administrations given by different verdure, nations focus on green drives to save normal living spaces, decrease deforestation, and advance reasonable land use rehearses. This responsibility stretches out to marine preservation, as countries try to shield seas and marine life from contamination, overfishing, and the effects of environmental change.

   Social contemplations likewise assume a critical part in spurring nations to focus on green drives. The acknowledgment that ecological debasement lopsidedly influences minimized networks, prompting issues like air and water contamination, highlights the civil rights part of manageability. Focusing on green drives lines up with a promise to guaranteeing impartial admittance to assets, clean conditions, and potential open doors for all portions of society.

2. **Methodologies for Carrying out Green Drives:**

   Nations utilize different techniques to carry out green drives, perceiving that a multi-layered approach is fundamental for successful and practical change. A typical technique includes setting aggressive targets and responsibilities, frequently cherished in public strategies or peaceful accords. These objectives might incorporate explicit objectives for fossil fuel byproducts decrease, sustainable power reception, and preservation endeavors.

   Interests in environmentally friendly power framework address a foundation of many nations' green drives. Sunlight based, wind, hydro, and geothermal energy projects add to decreasing dependence on petroleum derivatives, bringing down carbon impressions, and cultivating a progress to cleaner and more maintainable energy sources. Impetuses for organizations and people to embrace sustainable power innovations, like sunlight based chargers or electric vehicles, are in many cases vital parts of these methodologies.

   Green drives likewise envelop endeavors to upgrade energy effectiveness in different areas. This includes executing approaches and practices that diminish energy utilization, work on the productivity of structures and enterprises, and advance the utilization of energy-effective innovations. Building regulations, principles for energy-proficient machines, and public mindfulness crusades add to these endeavors.

Nations focus on reasonable transportation as a basic part of green drives. This includes interests in open transportation, the improvement of cycling and person on foot framework, and the advancement of electric vehicles. By empowering a shift towards supportable methods of transportation, countries intend to lessen air contamination, decline dependence on non-renewable energy sources, and make more decent and harmless to the ecosystem metropolitan spaces.

Practical agribusiness is one more key area of concentration inside green drives. Nations perceive the significance of advancing practices that focus on soil wellbeing, decrease compound information sources, and limit ecological effect. Agroecological approaches, accuracy cultivating, and natural cultivating rehearses add to building a more maintainable and strong farming area.

Nature-based arrangements, for example, afforestation and reforestation projects, assume an essential part in green drives. Perceiving the essential job of woodlands in carbon sequestration, biodiversity preservation, and environment guideline, nations focus on drives that reestablish and safeguard normal biological systems. These endeavors add to ecological objectives as well as help neighborhood networks and improve generally speaking biological system wellbeing.

Green money and supportable venture systems are necessary to the execution of green drives. Nations influence monetary instruments, for example, green securities and maintainable improvement assets, to prepare assets for eco-accommodating tasks. Empowering private area association in feasible ventures, adjusting monetary motivating forces to natural objectives, and coordinating ecological contemplations into monetary dynamic cycles add to the general progress of green money procedures.

3. **Effect and Advantages of Focusing on Green Drives:**

    The effect of nations focusing on green drives is multi-layered, prompting a scope of ecological, financial, and social advantages. One of the essential ecological advantages is the decrease of fossil fuel byproducts. Countries that focus on environmentally friendly power, energy productivity, and manageable practices add to relieving environmental change and bringing down the in general ecological impression.

    The preservation of biodiversity and rebuilding of biological systems address critical natural results of green drives. Afforestation projects, marine preservation endeavors, and supportable land the executives rehearses add to the safeguarding of biodiversity, safeguard jeopardized species, and upgrade by and large environment strength. Solid biological systems offer fundamental types of assistance like clean water, fertilization of harvests, and environment guideline.

Green drives groundbreakingly affect the energy area, encouraging a change to cleaner and more feasible sources. Nations that focus on environmentally friendly power projects diminish their reliance on petroleum products, decline air contamination, and add to a more economical and strong energy framework. The expansion of fuel sources improves energy security and mitigates the natural effect of conventional energy creation.

Financial advantages emerge from the development of green ventures and the formation of green positions. Interests in environmentally friendly power, reasonable transportation, and eco-accommodating advancements spike financial turn of events and development. The green economy creates work potential open doors in regions like clean energy creation, energy-effective development, and manageable horticulture. This tends to joblessness as well as encourages a progress to additional comprehensive and impartial monetary frameworks.

Economical farming practices, advanced through green drives, add to food security and flexibility even with environmental change. Agroecological approaches improve soil wellbeing, lessen the requirement for compound sources of info, and advance different and tough yield assortments. By focusing on maintainable horticulture, countries guarantee the drawn out suitability of their food frameworks and diminish the ecological effect of customary cultivating rehearses.

Green drives likewise have social advantages, especially with regards to general wellbeing. Decreases in air and water contamination, frequently connected with the change to cleaner energy sources and feasible transportation, lead to further developed air quality and better wellbeing results. Admittance to green spaces, advanced through supportable metropolitan preparation, adds to mental prosperity and personal satisfaction.

Inclusivity and social value are improved through green drives that focus on defenseless and minimized networks. The progress to maintainable practices guarantees that the advantages of ecological protection and green improvement are open to all fragments of society. This tends to social inconsistencies as well as cultivates a feeling of local area commitment and strengthening.

4. **Instances of Nations Focusing on Green Drives:**

   A few nations all over the planet have arisen as pioneers in focusing on green drives, exhibiting different methodologies and showing the plausibility of economical turn of events. One essential model is Denmark, prestigious for its obligation to environmentally friendly power. The nation has set aggressive focuses to be carbon-nonpartisan by 2050 and has put essentially in wind energy. Denmark's breeze energy area is a worldwide pioneer, with wind turbines providing a significant part of the nation's power.

   Germany is one more model in green drives, especially with regards to the energy progress known as the "Energiewende." The nation has made significant interests in sustainable power, including sun oriented and wind power. Germany's obligation to eliminating atomic power and lessening fossil fuel byproducts has situated it as a pioneer in the worldwide shift towards maintainable energy frameworks.

Costa Rica stands apart as a forerunner in natural protection and sustainable power reception. The nation has accomplished almost 100 percent sustainable power age, essentially from hydropower, wind, and geothermal sources. Costa Rica's devotion to saving its rich biodiversity is reflected in its broad public park framework and obligation to reforestation.

China, regardless of being a huge supporter of worldwide fossil fuel byproducts, has likewise focused on green drives as of late. The nation has set aggressive focuses for carbon nonpartisanship by 2060 and is putting vigorously in sustainable power, electric vehicles, and green advances. China's push for green improvement is viewed as a significant stage in addressing its natural difficulties and adding to worldwide manageability.

Bhutan's obligation to focusing on green drives is well established in its novel way to deal with estimating public achievement. The nation focuses on Gross Public Satisfaction over GDP (Gross domestic product) and has carried out arrangements to keep up with ecological manageability. Bhutan's emphasis on woods protection, carbon impartiality, and economical the travel industry epitomizes its commitment to all encompassing and maintainable turn of events.

5. **Difficulties and Contemplations:**

While nations focusing on green drives have shown estimable advancement, they additionally face difficulties and contemplations that warrant consideration. One normal test is the requirement for critical forthright interests in green foundation and advancements. The progress to sustainable power, maintainable transportation, and eco-accommodating practices frequently requires significant monetary assets, presenting difficulties for certain countries, particularly those with restricted financial limits.

The coordination of strategies and endeavors across various areas and levels of government is another test. Green drives frequently require cooperative activity between different partners, including government offices, confidential undertakings, and common society. Guaranteeing compelling correspondence, collaboration, and arrangement of interests among these elements is significant for the fruitful execution of green approaches.

Offsetting financial improvement with ecological safeguarding is a fragile errand. A few countries face the test of overseeing contending interests, especially when customary ventures, like non-renewable energy source extraction or escalated farming, are integral to their economies. Finding systems for a simply change that considers the government assistance of laborers and networks reliant upon these businesses is fundamental for exploring this test.

Worldwide collaboration and the exchange of green innovations are basic contemplations. Agricultural nations, specifically, may confront difficulties in embracing green drives without satisfactory admittance to advances and monetary assets. World-wide coordinated effort, monetary help, and innovation move instruments are vital for guaranteeing that the advantages of green advancement are shared internationally.

Tending to social value and guaranteeing that the advantages of green drives are comprehensive address continuous contemplations. Now and again, weak networks might bear unbalanced loads, like the possible removal of conventional vocations during the change to reasonable practices. Green strategies should be planned with a sharp consciousness of social effects and with components set up to limit imbalances.

Strategy soundness and long haul responsibility are fundamental for the outcome of green drives. Political advances or changes in administration can some of the time lead to shifts in needs, possibly affecting the coherence of supportability arrangements. Guaranteeing that green drives are implanted in long haul strategy systems and appreciate bipartisan help adds to strategy strength and powerful execution.

5.3 Balancing economic growth with environmental conservation

Offsetting financial development with natural preservation addresses quite possibly of the most squeezing and many-sided challenge confronting countries in the 21st hundred years. This sensitive balance includes exploring the frequently seen compromise between cultivating financial turn of events and protecting the climate. This thorough investigation digs into the intricacies, techniques, and ramifications of fitting monetary thriving with manageable natural practices.

1. **The Intricacies of Adjusting Financial Development and Ecological Protection:**

   The intricacies inborn in offsetting monetary development with ecological protection emerge from the verifiable worldview that financial advancement has frequently been inseparable from asset double-dealing and natural debasement. Conventional models of industrialization focused on quick monetary development, frequently to the detriment of environments, biodiversity, and normal assets. The multifaceted test lies in progressing from this worldview to a more maintainable and agreeable connection between financial exercises and ecological safeguarding.

   Globalization further convolutes this equilibrium as interconnected supply chains and the interest for assets drive financial exercises that can have broad ecological ramifications. The strain to meet the developing necessities of a thriving worldwide populace adds one more layer of intricacy, expecting countries to rethink conventional ways to deal with improvement.

   Urbanization, a sign of financial development, brings its own arrangement of difficulties. Quick metropolitan extension can prompt deforestation, loss of biodiversity, and expanded contamination. Adjusting the requirement for metropolitan improvement with ecological conservation turns into a basic thought in accomplishing maintainable development.

2. **Techniques for Orchestrating Monetary Development and Ecological Protection:**

1. **Green Development and Innovation:**

   Embracing green development and innovation addresses a vital system in accomplishing a harmony between monetary development and ecological protection. Progressions in environmentally friendly power, reasonable horticulture rehearses, and eco-accommodating advancements offer roads for financial improvement without the negative natural externalities related with customary ventures. Putting resources into innovative work to upgrade the proficiency and supportability of enterprises adds to encouraging monetary development while limiting natural effect.

2. **Roundabout Economy Practices:**

   Changing to a roundabout economy, where assets are utilized effectively, reused, and reused, presents a suitable procedure for reasonable turn of events. Roundabout economy rehearses limit squander age, advance asset preservation, and diminish the ecological impression of financial exercises. By decoupling monetary development from asset utilization, countries can accomplish thriving while at the same time relieving the consumption of regular assets and limiting contamination.

3. **Environment Based Approaches:**

   Integrating biological system based approaches into financial improvement methodologies is essential for keeping up with ecological equilibrium. Perceiving the worth of biological systems for water refinement, environment guideline, and biodiversity protection, countries can focus on strategies that shield basic living spaces and advance maintainable land use. This includes offsetting financial exercises with the safeguarding of normal scenes, guaranteeing that advancement doesn't think twice about trustworthiness of environments.

4. **Administrative Structures and Motivations:**

   Hearty administrative structures that implement natural norms and give motivators to maintainable practices are fundamental. Legislatures can assume a critical part in guaranteeing that monetary exercises comply with natural guidelines, advancing capable business lead. Impetus structures, for example, tax reductions for eco-accommodating drives or punishments for natural infringement, make a system where organizations are spurred to adjust their tasks to ecological protection objectives.

5. **Green Money and Speculation:**

   Utilizing green money instruments and economical speculation rehearses channels capital towards earth dependable tasks. Green bonds, ecological effect appraisals for speculation ventures, and supportability announcing add to adjusting financial development to natural contemplations. Empowering monetary organizations to consolidate natural, social, and administration (ESG) standards into their venture choices advances a more reasonable designation of capital.

6. **Local area Commitment and Training:**

Connecting with nearby networks in the dynamic cycle and encouraging ecological schooling are necessary parts of accomplishing a harmony between financial development and natural preservation. At the point when networks are engaged with information about supportable practices and have a voice being developed choices, there is a more prominent probability of accomplishing comprehensive and ecologically cognizant turn of events. Nearby help and mindfulness add to the outcome of preservation endeavors and maintainable drives.

3. Suggestions and Advantages of Adjusting Financial Development and Ecological Preservation:

1. **Long haul Financial Flexibility:**
   Accomplishing a harmony between financial development and natural preservation cultivates long haul monetary versatility. Economical practices alleviate the dangers related with natural corruption, asset consumption, and environmental change. By putting resources into green innovations and saving normal assets, countries assemble economies that are less powerless to shocks and interruptions, guaranteeing supported success for people in the future.

2. **Improved Worldwide Intensity:**
   Countries that focus on natural protection frequently get themselves more cutthroat on the worldwide stage. As global business sectors progressively esteem manageability, organizations that stick to eco-accommodating practices gain an upper hand. This draws in naturally cognizant buyers as well as positions countries as dependable worldwide entertainers, cultivating positive discretionary and exchange connections.

3. **Biodiversity Safeguarding:**
   Offsetting financial development with ecological preservation is instrumental in safeguarding biodiversity, which is fundamental for environment wellbeing and flexibility. Biodiversity gives biological system administrations like fertilization, soil fruitfulness, and infection guideline. Saving assorted biological systems adds to the maintainability of agribusiness, upholds food security, and improves in general environmental solidness.

4. **Worked on General Wellbeing:**
   Supportable advancement rehearses add to further developed general wellbeing results. Lessening air and water contamination, limiting openness to destructive synthetics, and advancing a perfect and solid climate lead to better wellbeing for populaces. Green spaces, economical metropolitan preparation, and the

reception of cleaner innovations add to alleviating wellbeing chances related with natural corruption.

5. **Environmental Change Moderation:**
Offsetting monetary development with natural preservation is an essential system for relieving the effects of environmental change. Ozone harming substance emanations from modern exercises add to an Earth-wide temperature boost and outrageous climate occasions. Progressing to environmentally friendly power, maintainable horticulture, and low-carbon advances assists countries with satisfying their responsibilities to worldwide environment arrangements, adding to worldwide endeavors to address environmental change.

6. **Social Value and Comprehensive Turn of events:**

Focusing on natural preservation in financial development systems adds to social value and comprehensive turn of events. Manageable practices guarantee that the advantages of financial development are appropriated evenhandedly among various portions of society. This incorporates contemplations for powerless and underestimated networks, elevating admittance to assets, and cultivating local area versatility even with ecological difficulties.

4. Challenges in Accomplishing Equilibrium:
Regardless of the advantages and methodologies, accomplishing a harmony between monetary development and ecological protection isn't without challenges.

1. **Momentary Financial Tensions:**
Transient monetary tensions frequently lead to choices that focus on quick acquires over long haul manageability. Monetary strategies equipped towards fast development might disregard natural contemplations, especially in circumstances where state run administrations face earnest financial difficulties.

2. **Political Will and Strategy Execution:**
The viability of natural arrangements relies upon political will and the capacity to execute guidelines. Political contemplations, campaigning from personal stakes, and difficulties in implementing guidelines can obstruct the fruitful reconciliation of ecological preservation into financial advancement plans.

3. **Worldwide Interconnectedness:**
The worldwide idea of financial exercises confuses endeavors to accomplish balance. Ecological effects related with worldwide inventory chains, worldwide exchange, and transboundary contamination require facilitated endeavors on a worldwide scale. The test lies in adjusting the needs of different countries to shifting degrees of monetary turn of events.

4. **Mechanical and Foundation Boundaries:**
A few countries might confront mechanical and foundation boundaries in embracing manageable practices. The progress to environmentally friendly

power, for instance, requires huge interests in framework and might be trying for nations with restricted assets. Worldwide participation and innovation move systems are fundamental in conquering these hindrances.

5. **Compromises and Hard decisions:**

Accomplishing balance frequently includes settling on tough choices and compromises. Finding some kind of harmony between financial development and ecological protection might require forfeiting specific monetary exercises that have critical natural effects. Choices about land use, asset extraction, and framework advancement frequently include compromises that require cautious thought.

Chapter 6

Reskilling and Workforce Adaptation

Reskilling and labor force variation have become basic despite quick mechanical progressions, advancing position scenes, and the extraordinary effect of worldwide occasions like the Coronavirus pandemic. This far reaching investigation dives into the difficulties, systems, and suggestions related with reskilling, underscoring the requirement for a dynamic and versatile labor force in the 21st 100 years.

1. **The Basic of Reskilling in a Unique Workplace:**

The contemporary workplace is portrayed by extraordinary changes, driven fundamentally by mechanical advancements and the rising joining of mechanization and man-made brainpower. The fast speed of progress delivers specific abilities out of date while provoking an interest for new, frequently innovation driven capabilities. The basic of reskilling emerges from the need to outfit the labor force with the abilities and information expected to effectively explore this powerful scene.

1. **Mechanical Disturbance:**
   The fourth modern transformation, set apart by progressions in regions, for example, man-made brainpower, AI, advanced mechanics, and the Web of Things, has upset conventional work jobs. Mechanization is reshaping enterprises, and errands that were once performed by people are presently being taken care of by machines. Reskilling becomes fundamental to adjust the labor force to the innovative moves and guarantee that people stay significant and employable.
2. **Globalization and Remote Work Patterns:**
   Globalization and the ascent of remote work have extended the opposition for occupations on a worldwide scale. Computerized network permits associations to take advantage of a worldwide ability pool, underscoring the requirement for laborers to have specialized abilities as well as the capacity to team up

across societies and work successfully in virtual conditions. Reskilling drives should include specialized abilities as well as diverse correspondence and distant coordinated effort abilities.

3. **Effect of the Coronavirus Pandemic:**

The Coronavirus pandemic has sped up specific labor force patterns, including remote work, digitalization, and the reception of online stages for cooperation. The pandemic highlighted the significance of computerized proficiency, versatility, and strength. Reskilling drives post-pandemic should address the developing idea of work and plan people for a future where adaptability and dexterity are vital.

2. **Challenges in Reskilling:**

1. **Ability Holes and Confuse:**
   Recognizing and tending to expertise holes is an essential test in reskilling endeavors. There is many times a befuddle between the abilities moved by the ongoing labor force and those requested by arising position jobs. Overcoming this issue requires an exhaustive comprehension of industry needs, compelling joint effort between instructive foundations and organizations, and proactive measures to expect future expertise necessities.

2. **Admittance to Instruction and Preparing:**
   Inconsistent admittance to schooling and preparing valuable open doors is a constant test in reskilling. Differences in view of financial elements, geological area, and instructive foundation can impede people's capacity to gain new abilities. Reskilling drives should focus on inclusivity, guaranteeing that open doors are available to people from assorted foundations and socioeconomics.

3. **Protection from Change:**
   Protection from change, both from people and associations, represents a huge test in reskilling endeavors. Representatives might be fearful about embracing new advancements or mastering new abilities, while associations might confront opposition in carrying out extensive reskilling programs. Beating this challenge requires successful change the executives methodologies, clear correspondence, and a culture that values persistent learning.

4. **Quick Innovative Progressions:**
   The speed of mechanical progressions presents a test in planning reskilling programs that stay pertinent over the long run. As new advances arise, the abilities requested by the gig market develop. Reskilling drives should be lithe, versatile, and prepared to address the fast changes in innovation to guarantee that the labor force stays on the ball.

5. **Long lasting Learning Society:**

Developing a culture of long lasting learning is a basic test. Conventional training models frequently accentuate learning in the beginning phases of life, however the powerful idea of work requests constant ability improvement. Reskilling drives need to impart a mentality of long lasting picking up, empowering people to proactively look for open doors for expertise improvement all through their vocations.

3. Procedures for Viable Reskilling:

1. **Cooperation among Instruction and Industry:**
   Successful coordinated effort between instructive organizations and ventures is pivotal for planning reskilling programs that line up with genuine work necessities. Industry input helps tailor instructive educational programs to meet current and future labor force needs, guaranteeing that reskilling endeavors are commonsense and straightforwardly relevant to the developing position scene.

2. **Customized Learning Pathways:**
   Perceiving that people have exceptional learning styles and inclinations, re-skilling projects ought to integrate customized learning pathways. Versatile learning stages, mentorship programs, and the combination of advances, for example, computerized reasoning can work with customized opportunities for growth custom-made to individual requirements and speed.

3. **Accentuation on Delicate Abilities:**
   While specialized abilities are fundamental, the meaning of delicate abilities couldn't possibly be more significant. Reskilling drives should accentuate the improvement of abilities like decisive reasoning, correspondence, joint effort, and versatility. These abilities are adaptable across different jobs and businesses, adding to the general flexibility and adaptability of the labor force.

4. **Web based Learning Stages and Microcredentials:**
   The ascent of web based learning stages and microcredentialing has democratized admittance to schooling and preparing. Reskilling endeavors can use these stages to contact a worldwide crowd, giving adaptable and available learning open doors. Microcredentials, which are compact, expertise explicit certificates, permit people to procure designated abilities without focusing on extended instructive projects.

5. **Government and Corporate Drives:**
   State run administrations and enterprises assume essential parts in driving re-skilling drives. State run administrations can carry out arrangements that boost reskilling, designate assets for preparing programs, and team up with private areas to recognize ability needs. Organizations can lay out inner reskilling programs, offer learning open doors to representatives, and establish a steady climate that values persistent advancing as an essential resource.

6. **Center around Computerized Education:**

Advanced proficiency is basic in the ongoing mechanical scene. Reskilling endeavors ought to remember areas of strength for a for improving computerized education, guaranteeing that people are capable in utilizing computerized devices, teaming up in virtual conditions, and exploring on the web stages. Computerized proficiency isn't just an expertise yet in addition an empowering influence for getting to a wide exhibit of instructive assets.

4. Ramifications of Reskilling for People and Associations:

1. **Professional success and Employer stability:**
   For people, reskilling presents potential open doors for professional success and expanded employer stability. Procuring new abilities improves employability and positions people as important resources in the labor force. Nonstop learning and variation to arising advances add to proficient development and flexibility in a cutthroat work market.

2. **Authoritative Deftness and Development:**
   Associations that focus on reskilling foster a culture of nimbleness and development. A talented and versatile labor force is better prepared to answer industry changes, mechanical headways, and market patterns. Reskilling drives empower associations to remain on the ball, cultivating a unique climate that supports imagination and the quest for new open doors.

3. **Ability Maintenance and Enrollment:**
   Reskilling drives assume a significant part in ability maintenance and enlistment. Workers are bound to remain with associations that put resources into their expert turn of events. Also, associations that offer hearty reskilling programs draw in top ability looking for amazing open doors for development and expertise improvement. Reskilling turns into an essential device in building and holding a high-performing labor force.

4. **Financial Seriousness:**

According to a macroeconomic viewpoint, reskilling adds to a country's monetary seriousness. A gifted and versatile labor force draws in worldwide speculations, invigorates financial development, and positions the country as a center point for advancement. Countries that put resources into reskilling drives are bound to explore monetary difficulties effectively and exploit arising potential open doors.

5. The Eventual fate of Reskilling:

1. **Coordination of Man-made reasoning in Learning:**
   The future of reskilling is entwined with the coordination of man-made reasoning (artificial intelligence) in learning stages. Computer based intelligence can customize growth opportunities, dissect individual learning designs, and suggest custom-made courses. Keen coaching frameworks and artificial intelligence

driven evaluations improve the adequacy of reskilling programs, furnishing people with designated and versatile learning open doors.

2. **Ascent of Virtual and Increased Reality:**
Virtual and expanded reality advances are ready to assume a critical part in reskilling. These vivid advances offer sensible recreations, permitting people to rehearse and refine their abilities in virtual conditions. Virtual study halls, increased reality preparing modules, and intuitive reproductions improve the reasonable relevance of reskilling drives.

3. **Shift towards Abilities Based Employing:**
As reskilling becomes essential to labor force improvement, there is a detectable shift towards abilities based recruiting. Bosses are putting more prominent accentuation on a singular's range of abilities and versatility as opposed to customary capabilities. Perceiving the developing idea of work, employing rehearses are turning out to be more spry, zeroing in on up-and-comers' capacities to contribute actually in powerful conditions.

4. **Nonstop Learning Environments:**

What's in store imagines the foundation of constant learning environments where people consistently progress between schooling, work, and reskilling open doors all through their professions. Long lasting learning becomes implanted in cultural standards, upheld by adaptable instructive designs, responsive ventures, and a culture that qualities and boosts nonstop expertise improvement.

6.1 Analysis of shifts in the job market post-pandemic

The Coronavirus pandemic has achieved remarkable disturbances to the worldwide economy, bringing about significant changes in the gig market.

This examination investigates the complex changes and patterns that have arisen in the post-pandemic work scene, analyzing the effect on ventures, remote work elements, abilities sought after, and the advancing boss representative relationship.

1. **Influence on Businesses and Areas:**
1. **Sped up Advanced Change:**
Perhaps of the most perceptible change in the post-pandemic work market is the sped up speed of advanced change across ventures. Associations that recently depended on customary models had to embrace innovation to guarantee business congruity during lockdowns. Subsequently, there is an uplifted interest for experts with skill in computerized advancements, distributed computing, network protection, and information examination.

2. **Internet business and Online Administrations Flood:**
The lockdowns and social separating estimates provoked a flood in web based business and online administrations. Retail, diversion, and schooling, among different areas, saw a quick change to computerized stages. This shift has

prompted expanded interest for experts in regions like advanced promoting, web based business the board, online substance creation, and network protection to address the difficulties related with the digitalization of administrations.

3. **Medical services and Biotechnology Development:**
   The pandemic highlighted the basic significance of the medical services and bio-technology areas. The interest for medical services experts, specialists, and drug specialists flooded. This pattern is probably going to endure as the attention on general wellbeing heightens, prompting expanded open positions in regions like the study of disease transmission, immunization advancement, telemedicine, and medical care innovation.

4. **Restored Accentuation on Fundamental Administrations:**

The pandemic featured the meaning of fundamental administrations, including operations, store network the board, and fundamental retail. Experts in coordinated operations and production network the board experienced expanded request as associations tried to fabricate versatile stock chains. Occupations in fundamental retail, especially in areas like staple and medical services, stayed steady and, surprisingly, experienced development.

2. Remote Work Elements:

1. **Expansion of Remote Work:**
   The pandemic incited an inescapable reception of remote work as a reaction to lockdowns and social separating measures. Numerous associations, at first constrained into remote work, found that it very well may be productive and financially savvy.
   Therefore, remote work has turned into a long-lasting installation for various ventures. This shift has suggestions for work searchers, who may now approach open doors past topographical imperatives.

2. **Cross breed Work Models:**
   The cross breed work model, consolidating remote work and office presence, has acquired notoriety. Associations perceive the worth of adaptability and are rethinking conventional work structures. Work jobs that consider remote or mixture work game plans are turning out to be progressively appealing to work searchers, impacting their decisions and inclinations. This shift additionally influences the kinds of abilities considered fundamental for far off joint effort and successful correspondence.

3. **Advanced Nomadism on the Ascent:**

The acknowledgment of remote work has led to the peculiarity of advanced nomadism. Experts are progressively deciding to work from a distance from various areas, frequently choosing a roaming way of life. This pattern has suggestions for the travel industry in areas that allure for computerized wanderers. Furthermore, bosses are adjusting their employing practices to oblige ability no matter what their actual area.

3. Abilities Popular:

1. **Advanced Proficiency and Innovation Abilities:**
   The sped up advanced change has increased the interest for computerized education and innovation abilities. Capability in computerized devices, information examination, man-made consciousness, and distributed computing is progressively viewed as a central necessity across different work jobs. Work searchers with a solid mechanical range of abilities are better situated to flourish in the developing position market.

2. **Flexibility and Versatility:**
   The vulnerabilities presented by the pandemic have highlighted the significance of flexibility and versatility. Bosses look for applicants who can explore change, embrace development, and flourish in powerful conditions. Work searchers who show the capacity to upskill, reskill, and turn in light of developing conditions are profoundly esteemed.

3. **Far off Joint effort and Correspondence:**
   The predominance of remote work has raised the significance of far off joint effort and relational abilities. Work searchers who can actually convey, team up, and oversee projects in virtual settings are popular. This remembers capability for virtual specialized devices, project the board programming, and the capacity to work consistently in a circulated group.

4. **The capacity to appreciate individuals on a profound level:**

As the idea of work develops, the significance of the ability to understand anyone on a deeper level has become more evident. Managers look for up-and-comers who can explore complex relational elements, grasp the feelings of partners, and encourage a good workplace. Work searchers who have compelling capacity to understand anyone on a profound level abilities are strategically situated for progress in group based and remote work settings.

4. Advancing Boss Worker Relationship:

1. **Center around Worker Prosperity:**
   The pandemic has provoked a reconsideration of the business representative relationship, with an expanded spotlight on worker prosperity. Associations are taking on arrangements that focus on emotional well-being, balance between fun and serious activities, and by and large health. Work searchers are progressively considering an association's obligation to representative prosperity while assessing likely managers.

2. **Adaptable Work Game plans as an Advantage:**

The acknowledgment of remote work has situated adaptable work game plans as a critical advantage. Managers offering adaptability concerning remote work choices, adaptable hours, and mixture work models are seen as appealing by work searchers. Adaptability has turned into a critical thought in the dynamic cycle for the two managers and workers.

3. **Nonstop Learning and Expert Turn of events:**
The accentuation on nonstop learning and expert improvement has increased. Businesses perceive the significance of upskilling and reskilling their labor force to remain cutthroat. Work searchers who focus on learning and improvement, search out valuable open doors for expertise upgrade, and show a promise to long lasting learning are pursued in the gig market.

4. **Accentuation on Variety, Value, and Incorporation:**

The uplifted familiarity with social issues has prompted an expanded accentuation on variety, value, and consideration in the work environment. Managers are effectively looking to construct different groups and establish comprehensive workplaces. Work searchers who focus on variety and incorporation contemplations and can add to encouraging a different working environment are progressively esteemed.

5. Difficulties and Contemplations:

1. **Tending to Imbalances in Remote Work:**
While remote work offers adaptability, it likewise presents difficulties connected with disparities. Not all occupation jobs can be performed from a distance, and certain socioeconomics may confront obstructions to getting to remote work valuable open doors.
Addressing these imbalances requires purposeful endeavors by managers to give admittance to remote work choices and make comprehensive arrangements.

2. **Offsetting Adaptability with Hierarchical Culture:**
Finding some kind of harmony between offering adaptability and keeping up with hierarchical culture is a test. Associations should guarantee that remote work strategies line up with the organization's qualities, and endeavors are made to encourage a firm group dynamic, even in virtual settings.

3. **Exploring Innovative Holes:**
The expanded dependence on innovation has uncovered mechanical holes, especially for people who might not approach the important devices or a steady web association. Spanning these holes is fundamental to guarantee equivalent open doors for all occupation searchers and workers, no matter what their mechanical assets.

4. **Alleviating Burnout and Exhaust:**

The obscuring of limits among work and individual life in distant settings has prompted worries about burnout and exhaust. Businesses need to execute measures to relieve these dangers, like setting clear assumptions, empowering breaks, and encouraging a culture that values balance between serious and fun activities.

6.2 Strategies for reskilling the workforce to meet evolving demands

The developing requests of the cutting edge labor force, driven by mechanical headways, changes in ventures, and the effect of worldwide occasions, require vigorous procedures for reskilling. Reskilling, the most common way of securing new abilities or improving existing ones to fulfill advancing needs, is essential for the two people and associations to flourish in powerful conditions. This complete investigation digs into key methodologies for powerful reskilling, taking into account the complex difficulties and potential open doors introduced by the quickly evolving scene.

1. **Extensive Abilities Appraisal:**
1. **Recognizing Ability Holes:**
   The most important phase in any fruitful reskilling procedure is an extensive abilities evaluation. Associations and people need to recognize existing expertise holes by assessing the ongoing range of abilities against the abilities requested by advancing position jobs. This appraisal fills in as the establishment for focused on reskilling endeavors, guaranteeing that assets are distributed to regions with the main holes.
2. **Future-Sealing Abilities:**

Past tending to quick expertise holes, a forward-looking methodology includes future-sealing abilities. Expecting to arise patterns in innovation, industry prerequisites, and market requests is pivotal. Associations ought to put resources into recognizing the abilities right now sought after as well as those prone to be fundamental later on. This proactive methodology limits the gamble of fast out of date quality and positions people and associations as coordinated and versatile.

2. **Custom fitted Learning Pathways:**

1. **Customized Learning Plans:**
   Reskilling endeavors ought to embrace customized learning pathways. Perceiving that people have extraordinary learning styles, inclinations, and beginning stages, customized learning plans take care of the particular necessities of every student. This approach might include modifying preparing programs, offering assorted learning configurations, and utilizing versatile learning advances that change content in view of individual advancement.
2. **Microlearning and Reduced down Modules:**
   The joining of microlearning and scaled down modules upgrades the viability of reskilling drives. Separating learning content into more modest, effectively edible units obliges occupied plans and works with consistent learning. Microlearning

additionally adjusts well to the inclinations of present day students, who frequently favor short, engaged eruptions of data over extensive instructive meetings.

3. **Mixed Learning Approaches:**

Consolidating conventional strategies with computerized and experiential learning makes a mixed learning approach. This system consolidates homeroom preparing, online courses, studios, and involved encounters to give a comprehensive and connecting with opportunity for growth. Mixed learning takes care of different learning styles, encourages coordinated effort, and considers adaptability in reskilling programs.

3. **Coordinated effort with Instructive Foundations:**

1. **Industry-The scholarly world Organizations:**
   Working together with instructive foundations is fundamental for adjusting reskilling endeavors with industry needs. Laying out associations among organizations and colleges or professional instructional hubs works with the advancement of educational plan that reflects certifiable prerequisites. Industry-the scholarly world joint efforts likewise make pathways for students to consistently change from schooling to business.

2. **Entry level position and Apprenticeship Projects:**
   Entry level position and apprenticeship programs overcome any issues between hypothetical information and pragmatic application. By giving active involvement with genuine workplaces, these projects upgrade the adequacy of reskilling. They offer an organized methodology for people to apply recently procured abilities, construct certainty, and gain openness to industry-explicit difficulties.

3. **Ceaseless Criticism Systems:**

Laying out ceaseless criticism systems among bosses and instructive organizations is significant for refining reskilling programs. Customary correspondence guarantees that Instructive substance stays important, lines up with industry drifts, and adjusts to the changing requirements of the gig market. This cooperative methodology encourages a biological system where it are dynamic and receptive to reskilling drives.

4. **Coordination of Innovation:**

1. **Computerized Learning Stages:**
   Utilizing computerized learning stages is fundamental to present day reskilling systems. Online courses, online classes, and virtual homerooms give adaptability and openness, permitting students to gain new abilities at their own speed and accommodation. Computerized stages likewise offer an abundance of assets,

including intelligent substance, recreations, and cooperative instruments that upgrade the opportunity for growth.

2. **Artificial intelligence Controlled Learning Frameworks:**
   The mix of man-made reasoning (man-made intelligence) in learning frameworks empowers customized and versatile opportunities for growth. Computer based intelligence calculations dissect individual learning designs, track progress, and suggest custom fitted substance. This innovation driven approach guarantees that reskilling endeavors are effective, designated, and lined up with the special requirements of every student.

3. **Virtual and Expanded Reality:**

Virtual and expanded reality advances offer vivid opportunities for growth. Especially important for expertise concentrated enterprises, these advances reenact genuine situations, permitting students to rehearse and refine their abilities in a virtual climate. From operations to specialized investigating, virtual and expanded reality add to the pragmatic utilization of reskilling drives.

5. Delicate Abilities Improvement:

1. **Accentuation on Capacity to understand anyone on a profound level:**
   Notwithstanding specialized abilities, reskilling systems ought to underline the improvement of delicate abilities, with a specific spotlight on capacity to understand individuals on a deeper level. The capacity to understand people at their core, enveloping mindfulness, sympathy, and compelling correspondence, is critical in cooperative workplaces. Preparing programs that support the capacity to appreciate people at their core add to upgraded relational connections and group elements.

2. **Decisive Reasoning and Critical thinking:**
   Decisive reasoning and critical thinking abilities are major in unique workplaces. Reskilling drives ought to integrate exercises that challenge students to investigate circumstances, think fundamentally, and foster creative arrangements. Contextual investigations, reproductions, and situation based learning add to the development of these fundamental abilities.

3. **Correspondence and Cooperation Preparing:**

Viable correspondence and cooperation are fundamental in remote and half and half work settings. Reskilling projects ought to incorporate modules that upgrade relational abilities, both verbal and composed, and advance compelling cooperation in virtual groups. Preparing in virtual joint effort apparatuses further gets ready people for the requests of present day workplaces.

6. Consistent Learning Society:

1. **Advancing a Development Outlook:**
   Encouraging a development outlook is primary to making a culture of constant learning. People and associations ought to embrace the conviction that capacities can be created through devotion and difficult work. This mentality shift supports an uplifting perspective toward moves and an eagerness to participate in continuous mastering and expertise improvement.
2. **Influential position Demonstrating:**
   Initiative assumes a critical part in forming the way of life of an association. At the point when pioneers effectively partake in and support ceaseless learning drives, it sets a strong model for workers. Pioneers who focus on their own reskilling show a pledge to remaining pertinent and establish a climate where consistent learning is esteemed at all levels.
3. **Acknowledgment and Compensations for Learning:**

Recognizing and compensating learning accomplishments supports a culture of consistent learning. Associations can execute acknowledgment projects, accreditations, or gamification components to celebrate achievements in reskilling ventures. These impetuses add to a positive learning society and propel people to take part in continuous improvement effectively.

7. Spryness in Adjusting to Arising Patterns:

1. **Customary Ecological Sweeps:**
   To guarantee the pertinence of reskilling endeavors, associations ought to direct standard ecological sweeps. This includes observing industry patterns, mechanical headways, and changes in market requests. By remaining informed about arising patterns, associations can adjust their reskilling methodologies to address advancing necessities and stay on the ball.
2. **Spry Reskilling Projects:**
   Lithe philosophies, ordinarily connected with programming advancement, can be applied to reskilling programs. Lithe reskilling includes iterative preparation, execution, and variation in light of criticism. This approach permits associations to rapidly answer evolving conditions, consolidate new advancements, and change learning needs progressively.
3. **Situation Anticipating What's to come:**

Taking part in situation arranging is a proactive technique for getting ready for future vulnerabilities. Associations can imagine different expected fates, recognize the abilities expected in every situation, and create reskilling plans as needs be. This forward-looking methodology positions associations to explore different likely prospects with readiness.

8. Comprehensive Reskilling Drives:

1. **Tending to Variety and Consideration:**
   Reskilling drives ought to be planned in view of variety and consideration. Associations need to think about the assorted foundations, encounters, and needs of their labor force. Guaranteeing that reskilling programs are available, comprehensive, and chivalrous of various learning styles adds to rise to potential open doors for all representatives.
2. **Available Learning Assets:**
   Openness is a vital thought in reskilling techniques. Giving learning assets in numerous configurations, obliging different abilities to learn, and offering support for people with assorted needs add to the inclusivity of reskilling drives. This approach guarantees that everybody, paying little heed to foundation or capacity, can effectively partake in learning programs.
3. **Emotionally supportive networks for Underrepresented Gatherings:**

Reskilling drives ought to incorporate designated emotionally supportive networks for underrepresented gatherings. This might include mentorship programs, organizing open doors, and extra assets to address explicit difficulties looked by specific socio-economics. Comprehensive reskilling drives add to making a labor force that reflects variety and advances value.

9. Estimating and Assessing Reskilling Effect:

1. **Laying out Key Execution Markers (KPIs):**
   Estimating the effect of reskilling drives requires the foundation of key execution markers (KPIs). KPIs might incorporate measurements, for example, expertise securing rates, use of new abilities in the working environment, and enhancements in generally crew execution. Clear KPIs give a quantifiable system to evaluating the outcome of reskilling programs.
2. **Criticism Circles and Constant Improvement:**
   Executing input circles is basic for constant improvement. Routinely assembling criticism from members, bosses, and different partners empowers associations to distinguish regions for development, change the substance and conveyance of reskilling programs, and guarantee continuous arrangement with hierarchical objectives and advancing industry needs.
3. **Connecting Reskilling to Authoritative Targets:**

The effect of reskilling endeavors is most significant when straightforwardly connected to authoritative targets. Adjusting reskilling programs with vital objectives guarantees that gained abilities add to the general outcome of the association. This association supports the benefit of reskilling as a vital piece of accomplishing more extensive business goals.

6.3 Addressing the challenges of unemployment and inequality

Tending to the complicated difficulties of joblessness and disparity requires complex methodologies that incorporate financial, social, and strategy aspects. These difficulties are interconnected, frequently worsening one another and presenting critical deterrents to comprehensive and manageable turn of events. This complete investigation dives into the complexities of joblessness and imbalance, inspecting their main drivers, results, and proposing techniques for moderation.

1. **Grasping the Elements of Joblessness:**
1. **Underlying and Repetitive Variables:**
   Joblessness is affected by both underlying and recurrent elements. Underlying joblessness is established in long haul shifts in the economy, for example, changes in innovation or industry rebuilding, prompting a confound between accessible positions and the abilities of the labor force. Repeating joblessness, then again, results from monetary slumps and downturns. Successful methodologies should address both primary and recurrent perspectives.
2. **Abilities Confound and Training Abberations:**

A basic part of joblessness is the confound between the abilities requested by the gig market and those moved by the labor force. Instruction inconsistencies intensify this issue, for certain people lacking admittance to quality schooling and preparing programs that line up with developing position necessities. Reskilling and upskilling drives are essential to overcoming this issue and guaranteeing that people are prepared for current and future work open doors.

2. **Facing the Underlying foundations of Disparity:**

1. **Financial Incongruities:**
   Financial imbalance is frequently sustained by abberations in pay and abundance dispersion. Major league salary workers gather abundance at a quicker rate, prompting a convergence of assets in the possession of a couple. Moderate tax assessment, impartial compensation arrangements, and social security nets are fundamental parts of endeavors to address monetary abberations.
2. **Segregation and Inclination:**

Segregation in view of orientation, race, identity, or different elements adds to imbalance in the work environment. Methodologies pointed toward encouraging variety and consideration, disposing of prejudicial practices, and advancing equivalent open doors are fundamental in making a fair work market. Organizations and policymakers assume a urgent part in executing and upholding antidiscrimination measures.

3. **Methodologies for Tending to Joblessness:**

1. **Far reaching Instruction Change:**

An upgrade of the schooling system is crucial to tending to joblessness. Accentuation ought to be put on creating abilities that line up with the requirements of the gig market. Professional preparation, apprenticeship projects, and organizations between instructive foundations and enterprises can guarantee that people are outfitted with the commonsense abilities requested by businesses.

2. **Reskilling and Long lasting Learning:**
Given the quick speed of innovative progressions, reskilling and long lasting learning are basic. Constant learning drives, both at the individual and authoritative levels, empower the labor force to adjust to changing position necessities. Businesses, instructive foundations, and state run administrations ought to team up to lay out open reskilling programs that take special care of assorted learning styles.

3. **Business and Private company Backing:**
Empowering business and supporting private companies add to work creation. Drives that give admittance to financing, mentorship, and assets for hopeful business visionaries can invigorate monetary action and produce work open doors. Legislatures can carry out arrangements that work with the development of independent companies and boost pioneering tries.

4. **Public Works Projects:**

During monetary slumps, public works projects can act as successful countermeasures to joblessness. Foundation projects, natural protection drives, and local area advancement programs make occupations as well as add to cultural prosperity. Legislatures can decisively put resources into projects that address both quick work needs and long haul improvement objectives.

4. Procedures for Alleviating Disparity:

1. **Moderate Tax assessment Approaches:**
Moderate tax collection, where higher pay workers are charged at a more prominent rate, is a vital device in tending to financial imbalance. This approach guarantees that the weight of tax assessment is proportionate to people's capacity to pay. Changes in charge strategies, including shutting escape clauses and forestalling tax avoidance, add to a more pleasant circulation of assets.

2. **Living Pay and Equivalent Compensation Drives:**
Executing living compensation approaches and advancing equivalent compensation for equivalent work are basic in tending to pay variations. Guaranteeing that all specialists get a compensation that covers their fundamental necessities adds to neediness decrease and encourages a more fair society. Straightforward compensation designs and measures to wipe out orientation and racial pay holes are fundamental parts of these drives.

3. **Social Security Nets and General Essential Pay:**

Laying out vigorous social security nets, including joblessness advantages, medical care, and lodging support, mitigates the effect of financial shocks and diminishes disparity. The idea of widespread essential pay (UBI) is acquiring consideration as a likely technique to give all residents an ordinary pay, independent of work status, guaranteeing a gauge way of life.

4. **Admittance to Quality Medical care and Instruction:**

Admittance to quality medical care and instruction is fundamental to tending to imbalance. Thorough medical care frameworks that are open to all add to worked on prosperity and can break the pattern of neediness. Furthermore, guaranteeing impartial admittance to quality training, from youth through advanced education, upgrades social versatility and adjusts open doors.

5. **Strategy Mediations:**

1. **Work Market Arrangements:**
   Work market strategies assume a significant part in molding business elements. States can execute strategies that advance work creation, safeguard laborers' freedoms, and guarantee fair work rehearses. Adaptability in labor markets ought to be offset with components that forestall double-dealing and assurance fair working circumstances.

2. **Comprehensive Monetary Strategies:**
   Monetary arrangements ought to be planned in light of inclusivity. Legislatures can focus on interests in areas that can possibly set out different work open doors. Comprehensive financial approaches consider the necessities of under-estimated networks and try to diminish abberations in admittance to assets and open doors.

3. **Reasonable Lodging Drives:**

Admittance to reasonable lodging is a critical figure tending to both joblessness and disparity. States can execute approaches that work with reasonable lodging drives, giving stable day to day environments to people and families. Reasonable lodging adds to local area strength and financial flexibility.

6. **Worldwide Participation and Exchange Strategies:**

1. **Fair Exchange Practices:**
   Global exchange strategies can affect homegrown business and imbalance. Upholding for fair exchange rehearses guarantees that worldwide financial connections focus on evenhanded dispersion of advantages. State run administrations ought to advance arrangements that forestall abuse of laborers in low-wage nations and advance fair work norms in worldwide stock chains.

2. **Worldwide Guide and Improvement:**

Worldwide participation as help and improvement drives is fundamental for tending to joblessness and imbalance on a more extensive scale.

Created countries can add to the financial advancement of less prosperous nations, encouraging position creation and diminishing worldwide monetary inconsistencies. Cooperative endeavors in schooling, medical care, and framework advancement add to reasonable advancement.

7. Innovative Consideration and Advanced Proficiency:

1. **Shutting the Computerized Separation:**
   The computerized partition compounds disparity, as admittance to innovation turns out to be progressively indispensable to financial support. Drives pointed toward shutting the advanced separation, including giving reasonable web access and gadgets, guarantee that people from all financial foundations can profit from the open doors introduced by the computerized economy.

2. **Advanced Education Projects:**

Couple with shutting the advanced separation, it is vital to advance computerized education. Advanced education programs furnish people with the abilities to explore online stages, take part in remote work, and influence computerized apparatuses for business venture. Computerized education is a critical part of reskilling endeavors to set up the labor force for the requests of the advanced time.

Chapter 7

Regional Perspectives on Recovery

The worldwide scene for financial recuperation is portrayed by different local viewpoints, molded by special financial elements, international elements, and the changed effects of the Coronavirus pandemic. Understanding these provincial points of view is essential for making powerful recuperation procedures and cultivating worldwide participation. This investigation dives into the unmistakable difficulties and amazing open doors looked by changed districts, featuring the complex idea of the recuperation interaction.

1. **North America:**

   North America, containing the US and Canada, presents a blended financial recuperation scene. The underlying shock of the pandemic incited quick government intercessions, including improvement bundles and money related approach measures. The U.S. Central bank carried out low-loan costs, supporting organizations and monetary business sectors. While the U.S. experienced vigorous bounce back in certain areas, like innovation and online business, others, similar to neighborliness and private ventures, confronted delayed difficulties. Canada, also, carried out significant monetary measures to counter the financial effect of the pandemic. Nonetheless, the recuperation has been lopsided, with areas like energy and the travel industry wrestling with relentless difficulties. The two nations accentuate immunization crusades as key to reestablishing purchaser certainty and monetary soundness. Cooperation between North American countries is imperative for adjusting recuperation techniques and tending to cross-line difficulties.

2. **Europe:**

   Europe confronted one of a kind difficulties with its multi-country structure, bringing about shifting recuperation directions. The European Association (EU) started an extensive recuperation plan, underlining fortitude among part states. The EU's NextGenerationEU program apportions significant assets for interests in digitalization, green change, and medical care. Southern European countries, intensely dependent on the travel industry, confronted serious monetary constrictions, while northern economies showed more noteworthy versatility.

The recuperation in Europe is intently attached to antibody appropriation, as far and wide immunization is seen as fundamental for resuming economies and working with cross-line travel. The EU's accentuation on a green change lines up with worldwide manageability objectives, introducing potential open doors for development and occupation creation. Composed endeavors to address monetary differences among part states and guarantee a bound together way to deal with recuperation are basic for Europe's supported financial restoration.

3. **Asia-Pacific:**

The Asia-Pacific district showed surprising versatility even with the pandemic, driven by compelling general wellbeing reactions and proactive monetary strategies. China, the world's second-biggest economy, bounced back quickly, exploiting homegrown utilization and hearty products. Different countries in the area, including Japan and South Korea, additionally showed monetary versatility, yet with changing levels of effect.

Asia-Pacific's recuperation account is molded by the district's unmistakable quality in worldwide stockpile chains, innovation, and assembling. The speed increase of computerized change, web based business, and progressions in innovation driven enterprises added to monetary recovery. Notwithstanding, challenges endure, especially for countries exceptionally reliant upon global the travel industry. Cooperative endeavors in the locale, like the Provincial Far reaching Monetary Organization (RCEP), further upgrade financial reconciliation and solidness.

4. **Latin America:**

Latin America confronted an intricate recuperation scene set apart by different financial designs and socio-political difficulties. The area experienced critical financial compressions, with nations like Brazil and Mexico wrestling with high disease rates and stressed medical care frameworks. Casual work markets, pervasive in numerous Latin American countries, heightened financial weaknesses during lockdowns.

While immunization crusades are in progress, the financial recuperation in Latin America is upset by primary issues, including elevated degrees of casual work, imbalance, and restricted admittance to medical care. States in the locale are zeroing in on friendly projects, designated upgrade measures, and financial broadening to encourage recuperation. Local coordinated effort is critical for tending to shared difficulties and utilizing aggregate qualities.

5. **Center East and North Africa (MENA):**

The MENA locale confronted a double shock from the pandemic and vacillations in oil costs, affecting both oil-trading and non-oil-sending out countries.

States carried out a scope of financial measures to relieve monetary difficulties, yet recuperation directions change across the locale. Nations with differentiated economies, for example, the Unified Bedouin Emirates, showed more noteworthy flexibility, while oil-subordinate countries confronted delayed financial strains.

MENA's recuperation is complicatedly connected to worldwide oil interest and international elements. Enhancement endeavors, especially in sustainable power and innovation, present open doors for financial change. Tending to youth joblessness, improving training, and encouraging development are key parts of the locale's recuperation methodologies. Provincial collaboration and security are essential for supported monetary recovery.

6. **Sub-Saharan Africa:**

Sub-Saharan Africa faced one of a kind difficulties following the pandemic, remembering restricted medical care foundation and weaknesses for the casual economy. The district experienced disturbances in key areas like agribusiness, the travel industry, and item sends out. Legislatures executed measures to alleviate the effect, however monetary requirements and restricted admittance to immunizations represented extra difficulties.

The recuperation in Sub-Saharan Africa is intently attached to antibody appropriation, monetary enhancement, and practical turn of events. Utilizing computerized innovations for monetary consideration, training, and medical care is a key concentration. Cooperative endeavors among African countries and worldwide help are crucial for tending to wellbeing incongruities, upgrading monetary strength, and cultivating comprehensive recuperation.

7. **Worldwide Participation and Difficulties:**

Worldwide participation is vital for tending to shared difficulties and cultivating a strong recuperation. The Admittance to Coronavirus Devices (ACT) Gas pedal and the COVAX drive intend to guarantee impartial admittance to immunizations around the world. Nonetheless, challenges persevere, including antibody dispersion differences, the requirement for obligation help in emerging countries, and the basic to adjust recuperation techniques to manageable advancement objectives.

Environmental change presents a worldwide test that requires facilitated endeavors. The Unified Countries System Show on Environmental Change (UNFCCC) and drives like the Paris Arrangement underline the significance of worldwide coordinated effort in relieving environment related dangers and encouraging feasible turn of events.

International strains, exchange debates, and the ascent of protectionist estimates present dangers to worldwide monetary solidness. Exploring these difficulties requires discretionary discourse, adherence to peaceful accords, and a guarantee to multilateralism.

7.1 Examination of unique challenges faced by different regions

The worldwide scene is portrayed by assorted and remarkable difficulties looked by changed areas, each wrestling with its own arrangement of financial elements, international elements, and the unmistakable effects of the Coronavirus pandemic. Understanding these difficulties is fundamental for creating focused on and compelling procedures custom-made to the particular necessities of every area. This assessment digs into the special difficulties defying different regions of the planet, revealing insight into the intricacy of the worldwide recuperation process.

1. **North America:**

   North America, containing the US and Canada, confronted particular difficulties in exploring the monetary repercussions of the pandemic. The underlying shockwave disturbed different areas, with unmistakable contrasts in the speed and nature of recuperation. The US, being the world's biggest economy, encountered a different recuperation scene. While specific areas, like innovation and internet business, flourished, others, including friendliness and independent companies, confronted delayed difficulties.

   The provincial difficulties in North America were intensified by the perplexing transaction of government and state reactions to the pandemic. Contrasting procedures, strategies, and immunization circulation plans added to an interwoven of recuperation directions. The cross-line monetary combination between the U.S. furthermore, Canada highlighted the significance of cooperative procedures to adjust recuperation endeavors and address shared difficulties.

2. **Europe:**

   Europe, portrayed by its different financial designs and multi-country elements, confronted an intricate recuperation scene. The European Association (EU) started an aggressive recuperation plan, underlining solidarity and fortitude among part states. Notwithstanding, challenges persevered, especially for Southern European countries intensely dependent on the travel industry. Variations in monetary flexibility among northern and southern economies highlighted the requirement for facilitated methodologies to connect financial holes.

   The complexities of recuperation in Europe were intently attached to the progress of immunization dissemination and the district's obligation to a green change. While the EU's NextGenerationEU program flagged a push toward supportability, monetary variations continued. Cooperative endeavors inside the EU were essential for guaranteeing a bound together methodology, tending to shared difficulties, and encouraging a comprehensive recuperation across the mainland.

3. **Asia-Pacific:**

   The Asia-Pacific district showed strength even with the pandemic, driven by powerful general wellbeing reactions and proactive monetary arrangements. China, a significant financial force to be reckoned with, bounced back quickly by gaining by homegrown utilization and strong commodities. In any case, recuperation directions fluctuated across the district, with countries like Japan and South Korea exhibiting flexibility, while others confronted difficulties.

One of the extraordinary difficulties in the Asia-Pacific area was the effect on worldwide stockpile chains. As a center for assembling and innovation driven ventures, disturbances in the store network resounded universally. The speed increase of computerized change and web based business introduced open doors for monetary restoration, however countries exceptionally reliant upon global the travel industry confronted delayed difficulties. Cooperative endeavors, like the Provincial Exhaustive Financial Association (RCEP), exhibited the significance of territorial coordination in conquering difficulties.

4. **Latin America:**

Latin America wrestled with a complicated recuperation scene set apart by different monetary designs and socio-political difficulties. The district confronted serious monetary compressions, especially in nations like Brazil and Mexico, where high disease rates stressed medical services frameworks. Casual work markets, predominant in numerous Latin American countries, heightened monetary weaknesses during lockdowns.

One of the exceptional difficulties in Latin America was the effect on casual economies and weak populaces. Legislatures carried out different financial measures, however underlying issues, including elevated degrees of casual work and imbalance, continued. Territorial coordinated effort became fundamental for tending to shared difficulties and utilizing aggregate qualities in beating financial differences.

5. **Center East and North Africa (MENA):**

The MENA district stood up to a double shock from the pandemic and variances in oil costs, affecting both oil-trading and non-oil-sending out countries. Legislatures carried out financial measures to alleviate monetary difficulties, however the recuperation directions changed. Broadened economies, for example, the Assembled Bedouin Emirates, showed more noteworthy flexibility, while oil-subordinate countries confronted delayed financial strains.

An exceptional test in the MENA district was the complicated connection between monetary recuperation, worldwide oil interest, and international elements. The district's expansion endeavors, especially in sustainable power and innovation, introduced open doors for monetary change. Tending to youth joblessness, improving training, and encouraging development became key parts of the area's recuperation procedures. Provincial collaboration and security were essential for supported monetary restoration.

6. **Sub-Saharan Africa:**

Sub-Saharan Africa faced exceptional difficulties following the pandemic, remembering restricted medical care framework and weaknesses for the casual economy. The district experienced disturbances in key areas like horticulture, the travel industry, and item sends out. Legislatures carried out measures to alleviate the effect, however financial limitations and restricted admittance to immunizations represented extra difficulties.

An unmistakable test in Sub-Saharan Africa was the effect on medical care frameworks and the requirement for far reaching immunization. Restricted admittance to antibodies, monetary broadening, and maintainable improvement became central focuses for recuperation. Utilizing computerized innovations for monetary consideration, schooling, and medical services arose as a key concentration, stressing the significance of cooperative endeavors among African countries and global help.

7. **Worldwide Participation and Difficulties:**

While every area confronted its extraordinary difficulties, worldwide participation stayed basic for tending to shared hindrances. Difficulties like immunization dispersion abberations, the requirement for obligation help in agricultural countries, and the basic to adjust recuperation techniques to reasonable improvement objectives highlighted the interconnected idea of the worldwide scene.

International strains, exchange debates, and the ascent of protectionist estimates presented dangers to worldwide monetary strength. Exploring these difficulties required discretionary exchange, adherence to peaceful accords, and a pledge to multilateralism. The Admittance to Coronavirus Apparatuses (ACT) Gas pedal and the COVAX drive planned to guarantee impartial admittance to antibodies around the world, yet challenges in execution persevered.

Environmental change introduced another worldwide test that necessary facilitated endeavors. The Unified Countries Structure Show on Environmental Change (UNFCCC) and drives like the Paris Arrangement accentuated the significance of global joint effort in moderating environment related dangers and cultivating practical turn of events.

7.2 Comparative analysis of regional recovery strategies

A similar examination of provincial recuperation techniques gives important bits of knowledge into the different methodologies embraced by various regions of the planet to defeat the monetary difficulties presented by the Coronavirus pandemic. Understanding the subtleties of these methodologies is fundamental for recognizing fruitful works on, gaining from inadequacies, and cultivating a cooperative worldwide recuperation. This examination looks at the particular recuperation techniques utilized across North America, Europe, the Asia-Pacific, Latin America, the Center East and North Africa (MENA), Sub-Saharan Africa, and evaluates the adequacy of each methodology.

1. **North America:**
   North America, containing the US and Canada, utilized a blend of financial and money related strategies to explore the monetary aftermath from the pandemic.

The US executed significant upgrade bundles, including direct installments to people and support for organizations. The Central bank assumed a vital part by keeping up with low-loan costs, giving liquidity, and supporting monetary business sectors. The recuperation, be that as it may, displayed sectoral inconsistencies, with innovation and internet business flourishing while areas like cordiality battled.

Canada additionally executed critical financial measures to counter the monetary effect. Notwithstanding, challenges continued, especially in areas vigorously subject to cross-line exchange and the travel industry. The two nations accentuated immunization crusades as key to reestablishing shopper certainty and monetary steadiness. The recuperation techniques highlighted the significance of hearty government mediations, designated upgrade measures, and cooperative endeavors among administrative and state substances.

2. **Europe:**

Europe, described by its different monetary designs and the European Association (EU), started a far reaching recuperation plan stressing fortitude among part states. The NextGenerationEU program allotted significant assets for interests in digitalization, green change, and medical services. Southern European countries vigorously dependent on the travel industry confronted serious financial withdrawals, while northern economies exhibited more noteworthy versatility.

The recuperation in Europe was intently attached to immunization circulation, with the EU underlining a brought together methodology. The EU's obligation to a green change introduced open doors for practical turn of events and development. Nonetheless, challenges continued, featuring the requirement for composed techniques to address monetary incongruities and guarantee a decent recuperation across the mainland.

3. **Asia-Pacific:**

The Asia-Pacific district exhibited surprising strength, driven by powerful general wellbeing reactions and proactive financial arrangements. China, a significant financial player, bounced back quickly by gaining by homegrown utilization and vigorous commodities. Different countries in the district, like Japan and South Korea, additionally showed monetary strength, despite the fact that difficulties fluctuated.

One of the prominent parts of the Asia-Pacific recuperation was the locale's unmistakable quality in worldwide stock chains and innovation driven enterprises. Computerized change and headways in innovation assumed a urgent part in monetary restoration. Notwithstanding, challenges persevered for countries exceptionally reliant upon global the travel industry. Cooperative endeavors, exemplified by the Territorial Complete Monetary Organization (RCEP), underscored provincial coordination as a critical driver of strength and recuperation.

4. **Latin America:**

Latin America confronted an intricate recuperation scene set apart by different monetary designs and socio-political difficulties. The area experienced critical financial compressions, especially in nations like Brazil and Mexico, where high disease rates stressed medical services frameworks. The pervasiveness of casual work markets increased financial weaknesses during lockdowns.

Legislatures in Latin America carried out different monetary measures, however underlying issues, including elevated degrees of casual work and disparity, continued. The remarkable test of casual economies expected designated procedures to help weak populaces. Territorial joint effort became fundamental for addressing shared difficulties and utilizing aggregate qualities to beat financial inconsistencies.

5. **Center East and North Africa (MENA):**
   The MENA district confronted a double shock from the pandemic and variances in oil costs, influencing both oil-trading and non-oil-sending out countries. Enhanced economies, for example, the Unified Middle Easterner Emirates, showed more prominent strength, while oil-subordinate countries confronted delayed financial strains. The multifaceted connection between monetary recuperation, worldwide oil interest, and international elements added intricacy to the locale's recuperation methodologies.

   MENA's enhancement endeavors, especially in sustainable power and innovation, introduced open doors for financial change. Tending to youth joblessness, improving training, and encouraging development were vital parts of the area's recuperation procedures. Provincial collaboration and soundness arose as key points of support for supported financial recovery in a locale set apart by different monetary designs and international intricacies.

6. **Sub-Saharan Africa:**
   Sub-Saharan Africa faced remarkable difficulties, remembering restricted medical care foundation and weaknesses for the casual economy. Disturbances in key areas like farming, the travel industry, and ware sends out presented huge difficulties. Legislatures executed measures to moderate the effect, yet monetary limitations and restricted admittance to immunizations introduced extra obstacles.

   One of the unmistakable difficulties in Sub-Saharan Africa was the effect on medical care frameworks and the requirement for far reaching immunization. Restricted admittance to immunizations, financial expansion, and economical improvement became central focuses for recuperation. Utilizing computerized innovations for monetary consideration, instruction, and medical services arose as a key concentration, underscoring the significance of cooperative endeavors among African countries and worldwide help.

7. **Worldwide Participation and Difficulties:**

While every district carried out remarkable recuperation methodologies, worldwide participation stayed crucial for tending to shared deterrents. Difficulties like immunization appropriation differences, the requirement for obligation alleviation in agricultural countries, and the basic to adjust recuperation procedures to practical improvement objectives highlighted the interconnected idea of the worldwide scene.

International pressures, exchange questions, and the ascent of protectionist estimates presented dangers to worldwide monetary solidness. Exploring these difficulties required strategic exchange, adherence to peaceful accords, and a guarantee to multilateralism. Drives like the Admittance to Coronavirus Apparatuses (ACT) Gas pedal and the COVAX drive meant to guarantee evenhanded admittance to immunizations around the world, featuring the significance of worldwide joint effort in conquering shared wellbeing challenges.

Near Investigation:

The near examination of territorial recuperation systems uncovers the two shared traits and divergences in approaches. Strong government mediations, monetary improvement, and immunization crusades arose as consistent ideas across locales. Notwithstanding, the viability of these procedures changed in view of the remarkable difficulties every area confronted.

In locales where innovation and online business assumed a critical part, for example, North America and portions of the Asia-Pacific, computerized change arose as a vital driver of recuperation. Cooperation inside local coalitions, as found in Europe and the Asia-Pacific, displayed the significance of facilitated endeavors in beating difficulties and utilizing aggregate qualities.

Districts with a high reliance on global the travel industry, similar to Europe and portions of Latin America, confronted delayed difficulties, featuring the requirement for broadened monetary techniques. The significance of maintainable turn of events, green advances, and developments in innovation were repeating topics across areas, accentuating the worldwide shift toward stronger and comprehensive economies.

The MENA locale's recuperation techniques were complicatedly connected to worldwide oil interest, highlighting the area's requirement for financial expansion. Sub-Saharan Africa confronted special difficulties connected with medical services foundation, immunization access, and the significance of utilizing advanced innovations for comprehensive turn of events.

Worldwide participation, as proven by drives like the COVAX drive, exhibited the acknowledgment of shared difficulties and the need for cooperative arrangements. In any case, challenges in execution, antibody conveyance variations, and international pressures featured the intricacy of cultivating genuine worldwide cooperation.

7.3 Opportunities for cross-regional collaboration

Valuable open doors for cross-provincial coordinated effort present an extraordinary pathway for tending to worldwide difficulties, encouraging financial recuperation, and building a stronger, interconnected world. As the Coronavirus pandemic has highlighted the requirement for aggregate activity, looking at the amazing open doors for joint effort across different areas uncovers expected roads for shared development, advancement, and reasonable turn of events. This investigation digs into the critical open doors for cross-territorial coordinated effort and their possible effect on world-wide financial recuperation.

1. **Shared Ability and Best Practices:**
   One of the essential open doors for cross-provincial coordinated effort lies in the sharing of aptitude and best practices. Various locales have experienced one of a kind provokes and contrived creative answers for address them. Cooperative stages for information trade can work with the exchange of fruitful techniques, whether in overseeing general wellbeing emergencies, carrying out successful monetary approaches, or cultivating reasonable turn of events.

   For example, a district that succeeds in computerized development can impart its encounters to others looking to improve their mechanical capacities. Essentially, locales that have effectively explored medical services difficulties can offer experiences into viable general wellbeing reactions. This cross-fertilization of thoughts and encounters adds to a worldwide information base, empowering districts to gain from one another's triumphs and disappointments, at last encouraging more viable and informed direction.

2. **Exchange and Monetary Mix:**
   Cross-territorial coordinated effort gives a valuable chance to reinforce exchange and financial reconciliation, making cooperative energies that advantage taking part locales. Territorial economic alliance, like the European Association (EU) and the Local Complete Financial Organization (RCEP) in Asia, epitomize the potential for monetary cooperation. By lessening exchange obstructions, fitting guidelines, and advancing the free progression of labor and products, areas can take advantage of one another's assets, improve efficiency, and animate monetary development.

   Moreover, cultivating monetary joining across areas can prompt the improvement of worldwide store network versatility. As seen during the pandemic, disturbances in a single locale can have flowing impacts on the worldwide economy. Cooperative endeavors to broaden and reinforce supply chains can moderate dangers and add to the soundness of the interconnected worldwide monetary framework.

3. **Advancement and Innovation Move:**
   Cross-provincial coordinated effort fills in as an impetus for development and innovation move. Various areas have special qualities and abilities in different enterprises, and cooperative drives consider the sharing of mechanical progressions and developments. For example, a locale known for its progressions in environmentally friendly power can team up with others trying to change to additional economical practices.

   Innovation move can reach out past natural drives to regions like medical services, schooling, and assembling. By working with the trading of mechanical ability, locales can on the whole address difficulties, upgrade efficiency, and drive financial turn of events. Joint innovative work drives, worldwide innovation centers, and cooperative advancement organizations can arise as useful assets for utilizing the qualities of different locales.

4. **Environmental Change Relief and Supportability:**
Tending to environmental change and advancing supportability address squeezing worldwide difficulties that require cross-territorial coordinated effort. Locales confronting comparative natural issues, for example, rising ocean levels, outrageous climate occasions, or biodiversity misfortune, can share experiences and team up on complete arrangements. Drives like the Paris Arrangement highlight the significance of composed endeavors to relieve the effect of environmental change.

Coordinated effort on maintainable advancement objectives can include sharing sustainable power innovations, carrying out preservation drives, and creating strong framework. Districts with mastery in maintainable practices, like roundabout economies or green money, can cooperate with others to speed up the worldwide change to a more reasonable and eco-accommodating future.

5. **Medical care and Pandemic Readiness:**
The Coronavirus pandemic has featured the basic significance of cross-local coordinated effort in medical services and pandemic readiness. Districts that have successfully dealt with the pandemic can share their encounters, systems, and medical care developments with those confronting progressing difficulties. Cooperative endeavors in immunization dissemination, clinical examination, and general wellbeing foundation can add to a more planned worldwide reaction to future wellbeing emergencies.

Moreover, joint drives in innovative work can prompt the disclosure of new therapies, drugs, and clinical advances. Making systems for the quick trade of data, information, and clinical skill can improve worldwide pandemic readiness, guaranteeing a swifter and more compelling reaction to arising wellbeing dangers.

6. **Social and Instructive Trade:**
Cross-local coordinated effort stretches out past monetary and innovative domains to include social and instructive trade. Areas can profit from common figuring out, cultivating social variety, and advancing instructive open doors. Drives that work with understudy trades, joint scholarly projects, and far-reaching developments add to a more interconnected world.

Social and instructive trade not just improves social orders by presenting people to assorted points of view yet additionally lays the foundation for future coordinated efforts. Interconnected worldwide residents with a profound comprehension of one another's societies are better prepared to team up on different fronts, from undertakings to strategic drives, encouraging a feeling of shared liability regarding worldwide difficulties.

7. **Framework Advancement and Availability:**
Coordinated effort on framework advancement and availability projects presents huge open doors for locales to upgrade their financial ties and work on in general network. Cross-territorial ventures, for example, transportation organizations, energy matrices, and computerized foundation, can work with the development of products, administrations, and data, making a more coordinated worldwide economy.

Drives like China's Belt and Street Drive embody the potential for cross-territorial framework joint effort. By connecting locales through an organization of transportation and energy projects, nations can use shared assets and improve monetary participation. Foundation joint effort animates monetary development as well as adds to the advancement of manageable and versatile networks.

8. **Discretionary and International Participation:**

Cross-provincial joint effort can possibly cultivate discretionary and international participation, adding to a more steady and secure worldwide climate. Districts can cooperate on political drives, compromise, and emergency the board. Cooperative endeavors in political discussions, like the Unified Countries, give stages to tending to shared difficulties and advancing harmony.

Besides, cross-local participation can act as an offset to international pressures, advancing discourse and understanding. Shared interests in provincial strength, monetary success, and ecological manageability can rise above political contrasts, prompting more compelling conciliatory connections and worldwide administration structures.

Chapter 8

Future Outlook and Global Economic Resilience

The future viewpoint and worldwide financial strength are basic contemplations as the world explores the post-pandemic scene and gets ready for future difficulties. The Coronavirus pandemic has highlighted the interconnectedness of economies, the significance of cooperative reactions, and the requirement for versatile systems to assemble flexibility. This investigation digs into the expected future patterns, challenges, and the basic for cultivating worldwide monetary versatility.

1. **Expected Future Patterns:**
1. **Advanced Change:** The sped up speed of computerized change saw during the pandemic is supposed to keep forming the future monetary scene. Ventures across areas, from money to medical services and assembling, are probably going to focus on advanced innovations. The joining of man-made reasoning, blockchain, and the Web of Things will reclassify business processes, upgrade proficiency, and add to financial development.
2. **Economical Turn of events:** The worldwide accentuation on maintainability is expected to develop, with a rising spotlight on green drives, sustainable power, and harmless to the ecosystem rehearses. States, organizations, and purchasers are probably going to drive interest for manageable items and administrations, prompting the improvement of green advances and the change to round economies. Feasible improvement objectives will become vital to monetary procedures, lining up with worldwide endeavors to battle environmental change.
3. **Strong Stock Chains:** The disturbances saw in worldwide stock chains during the pandemic have highlighted the requirement for versatility. Future patterns are supposed to focus on differentiated and strong stockpile chains. Regionalization, nearshoring, and the joining of computerized advancements to upgrade inventory network perceivability and dexterity will become key procedures to moderate dangers related with disturbances.
4. **Remote Work and Cross breed Models:** The experience of broad remote

work during the pandemic is probably going to impact future work models. Half breed work courses of action, joining remote and on location work, are supposed to turn out to be more pervasive. This shift has suggestions for urbanization designs, with expected influences on land, transportation, and the general construction of urban areas.

5. **Medical care Development:** The pandemic has sped up advancement in medical care, with progressions in telemedicine, antibody improvement, and computerized wellbeing arrangements. What's to come is probably going to observe proceeded with interests in medical care advancements, expanded worldwide cooperation on pandemic readiness, and an elevated spotlight on general wellbeing framework.

6. **Global Coordinated effort and Diplomacy:** The requirement for worldwide coordinated effort, both in tending to quick difficulties and cultivating long haul strength, is expected to turn out to be more articulated. Discretionary endeavors and worldwide participation will be essential in exploring complex international elements, tending to worldwide dangers, and guaranteeing fair admittance to assets, including antibodies and medical services.

2. Difficulties to Worldwide Monetary Flexibility:

1. **Disparity:** Diligent monetary imbalances inside and between nations represent a huge test to worldwide financial flexibility. The pandemic has exacerbated differences, with weak populaces confronting unbalanced influences. Tending to disparity requires deliberate endeavors in schooling, medical care, and social arrangements to guarantee comprehensive financial turn of events.

2. **Obligation and Financial Difficulties:** Numerous nations have brought about critical obligation to carry out boost measures and address the monetary aftermath of the pandemic. The test lies in dealing with this obligation trouble while supporting monetary recuperation. Monetary strategies should figure out some kind of harmony between supporting recuperation and keeping up with financial supportability.

3. **International Strains:** Continuous international pressures and exchange questions present dangers to worldwide monetary steadiness. Protectionist measures and exchange hindrances can prevent financial recuperation and disturb worldwide stockpile chains. Exploring these pressures requires political exchange, adherence to peaceful accords, and a promise to multilateralism.

4. **Environmental Change Dangers:** Environmental change presents both natural and financial dangers. The rising recurrence and power of outrageous climate occasions can upset supply chains, influence farming, and lead to financial misfortunes. Relieving environmental change gambles requires worldwide collaboration, manageable practices, and interests in strength.

5. **Innovative Disturbances:** While advanced change presents open doors, it likewise brings difficulties, including position relocation, network safety dangers, and moral contemplations. Dealing with the effect of mechanical interruptions on business and guaranteeing mindful development are basic for long haul monetary flexibility.

6. **Worldwide Wellbeing Dangers:** The continuous gamble of worldwide wellbeing dangers, including the possible development of new pandemics, requires supported readiness and cooperative endeavors. Reinforcing medical care frameworks, putting resources into innovative work, and further developing worldwide wellbeing administration are fundamental parts of building versatility against future wellbeing emergencies.

3. Building Worldwide Monetary Flexibility:

1. **Comprehensive Financial Approaches:** To address imbalance, legislatures and worldwide associations should carry out comprehensive monetary arrangements. This incorporates designated social projects, interests in training and medical services, and measures to enable minimized networks. Comprehensive development adds to social soundness and fabricates an establishment for versatile economies.

2. **Obligation The board and Monetary Approaches:** Viable obligation the executives and reasonable financial strategies are significant for supporting financial recuperation. Nations need to foster procedures to oversee obligation levels, investigate inventive funding instruments, and guarantee financial manageability. Facilitated endeavors at the worldwide level, including obligation help drives for emerging countries, can add to steadiness.

3. **Multilateralism and Strategy:** Reinforcing multilateralism and political endeavors is fundamental for tending to international strains and exchange questions. Cooperative ways to deal with worldwide administration, adherence to global standards, and conciliatory discourse are instrumental in encouraging a steady and helpful worldwide climate.

4. **Environment Versatility:** Building strength against environmental change requires worldwide collaboration on moderation and transformation systems. This remembers ventures for manageable foundation, the progress to sustainable power sources, and peaceful accords to lessen fossil fuel byproducts. Coordinating environment contemplations into financial strategies is fundamental for long haul flexibility.

5. **Innovative Morals and Guideline:** To oversee mechanical disturbances, an emphasis on moral contemplations and administrative systems is critical. Legislatures and businesses need to work cooperatively to lay out rules for capable

development, address network safety challenges, and guarantee that innovative headways benefit society at large.

6. **Worldwide Wellbeing Collaboration:** Fortifying worldwide wellbeing participation includes putting resources into medical care framework, supporting innovative work, and working on the availability of antibodies and clinical advances. Global associations, legislatures, and confidential areas need to team up on readiness gauges and guarantee impartial admittance to medical services assets.

8.1 Reflection on the progress made in the post-pandemic recovery

A reflection on the headway made in the post-pandemic recuperation reveals a perplexing and complex scene formed by the exchange of monetary, social, and worldwide elements. As countries endeavor to rise up out of the uncommon difficulties presented by the Coronavirus pandemic, evaluating the direction of recuperation becomes fundamental. This investigation dives into key parts of post-pandemic recuperation, including monetary restoration, cultural variations, and the job of global cooperation.

1. **Financial Recovery and Flexibility:**
1. **Worldwide Financial Patterns:** The post-pandemic recuperation has seen a steady yet lopsided monetary restoration across the globe. Different areas and nations have shown strength, adjusting to the developing monetary scene. While certain economies have bounced back quickly, determined by vigorous monetary measures and powerful immunization crusades, others keep on wrestling with difficulties, especially in areas intensely affected by limitations and disturbances.
2. **Sectoral Inconsistencies:** The recuperation progress has been set apart by eminent sectoral variations. Businesses like innovation, online business, and environmentally friendly power have shown amazing flexibility and, surprisingly, sped up development, utilizing computerized change and maintainability patterns. Interestingly, areas like cordiality, the travel industry, and independent ventures confronted delayed difficulties, featuring the requirement for designated help and versatile procedures.
3. **Work Market Elements:** The post-pandemic work market mirrors a moving worldview, with remote work and adaptable game plans turning out to be more common. While certain ventures have encountered work deficiencies, others wrestle with persevering joblessness. Reskilling and upskilling drives have acquired noticeable quality as people and organizations adjust to advancing position market requests, underscoring the significance of labor force dexterity in the recuperation cycle.
4. **Inflationary Tensions:** Inflationary tensions have arisen as a huge worry in the

post-pandemic recuperation. Store network disturbances, expanded interest for labor and products, and rising ware costs have added to inflationary patterns in different economies. National banks wrestle with the sensitive undertaking of offsetting monetary upgrade measures with the need to control expansion, exploring a mind boggling territory to guarantee economical development.

2. Cultural Variations and Changes:

1. **Remote Work and Half and half Models:** One of the outstanding cultural variations post-pandemic has been the change of work models. Remote work, once required by lockdowns, has developed into a more long-lasting component for some associations. Cross breed work models, consolidating remote and on location work, have become progressively predominant, reshaping the elements of working environment culture and testing conventional ideas of office-based business.

2. **Computerized Change:** The pandemic has catalyzed a significant advanced change across different parts of society. From medical care to schooling and amusement, advanced innovations have become indispensable to day to day existence. Telemedicine, internet learning stages, and computerized specialized devices have worked with progression during the pandemic as well as prepared for an additional digitized and interconnected future.

3. **Wellbeing and Prosperity Prioritization:** The uplifted familiarity with wellbeing and prosperity directly following the pandemic has incited people and social orders to focus on preventive measures and all encompassing ways to deal with wellbeing. Emotional well-being mindfulness, specifically, has acquired conspicuousness, prompting expanded promotion for psychological well-being backing, destigmatization, and the joining of psychological well-being contemplations into more extensive general wellbeing systems.

4. **Buyer Conduct Movements:** Purchaser conduct has gone through critical movements, impacted by evolving needs, monetary vulnerabilities, and developing assumptions. Web based business has seen phenomenal development, mirroring an inclination for internet shopping and contactless exchanges. Supportability contemplations have likewise impacted purchaser decisions, with a developing accentuation on eco-accommodating items and moral strategic policies.

3. Global Cooperation and Difficulties:

1. **Immunization Conveyance and Access:** Worldwide coordinated effort in immunization dissemination has been a crucial part of the post-pandemic recuperation. Drives like COVAX intended to guarantee evenhanded admittance to immunizations around the world. Be that as it may, challenges in circulation

variations, antibody reluctance, and worldwide antibody creation limit have highlighted the intricacies of accomplishing broad vaccination.

2. **Financial Incongruities and Obligation Help:** Tending to monetary inconsistencies among countries has been a point of convergence of worldwide coordinated effort. Calls for obligation help for emerging countries, monetary help systems, and endeavors to overcome any issues in admittance to financial open doors have featured the significance of an aggregate reaction to worldwide monetary difficulties.

3. **Environmental Change Moderation:** Global endeavors to alleviate environmental change have picked up speed in the post-pandemic time. The basic to work back better and cultivate practical improvement lines up with worldwide drives like the Paris Understanding. Cooperative undertakings to progress to sustainable power, decrease fossil fuel byproducts, and adjust to the effects of environmental change mirror a common obligation to natural stewardship.

4. **Worldwide Wellbeing Administration:** The pandemic has incited conversations about the requirement for reinforced worldwide wellbeing administration. Calls for improving worldwide wellbeing associations and laying out additional powerful systems for composed reactions to wellbeing emergencies highlight the acknowledgment of the interconnectedness of worldwide wellbeing and the need for cooperative structures.

4. Difficulties and Examples Learned:

1. **Persevering Difficulties:** Notwithstanding progress in post-pandemic recuperation, tenacious difficulties remain. Progressing vulnerabilities connected with new variations of the infection, international strains, and developing financial elements establish a climate where flexibility and strength stay vital. Tending to primary imbalances, especially in medical services and training, is a perplexing and progressing task that requires supported endeavors.

2. **Example in Readiness:** The pandemic has filled in as a distinct illustration in the significance of worldwide readiness for wellbeing emergencies. The requirement for strong medical services foundation, fast reaction systems, and worldwide collaboration in innovative work has become clear. Putting resources into pandemic readiness and reinforcing medical care frameworks are basic important points from the difficulties presented by Coronavirus.

3. **The Job of Innovation:** The groundbreaking job of innovation in empowering progression during emergencies and driving development in different areas has turned into a focal topic in the post-pandemic recuperation. Saddling the capability of computerized innovations for monetary development, medical care conveyance, and cultural network is an example that highlights the significance of embracing mechanical headways.

4. **Strength and Flexibility:** The capacity of social orders, organizations, and people to adjust and show versatility has been a critical focus point from the post-pandemic recuperation. The ability to explore vulnerabilities, embrace change, and develop notwithstanding difficulties has turned into a principal quality of fruitful recuperation endeavors.

5. Looking Forward:

1. **Proceeded with Variation:** The direction of post-pandemic recuperation proposes a scene described by proceeded with variation and change. Social orders and economies should explore developing difficulties, embrace advancement, and cultivate versatility. The continuous coordination of computerized advances, the redefinition of work models, and the prioritization of wellbeing and supportability will shape the future scene.
2. **Worldwide Participation:** The basic for worldwide collaboration stays key to tending to shared difficulties. Cooperative endeavors in antibody conveyance, environmental change alleviation, and financial inclusivity epitomize the inter-connected idea of worldwide issues. Reinforcing global joint effort systems and cultivating discretionary discourse are fundamental parts of building a stronger and helpful world.
3. **Maintainable Advancement Objectives:** The post-pandemic period gives a chance to rethink needs and adjust recuperation endeavors to supportable improvement objectives. Offsetting monetary development with ecological stewardship, tending to social disparities, and advancing comprehensive im-provement are essential to making a future that is both versatile and reasonable.
4. **Embracing Development:** The job of advancement in driving monetary advancement and cultural prosperity couldn't possibly be more significant. Embracing development across areas, from medical services to training and then some, will be essential for tending to arising difficulties and opening new open doors. States, organizations, and people the same are ready to add to a future portrayed by consistent development and flexibility.

8.2 Identification of potential risks and vulnerabilities

The ID of possible dangers and weaknesses in the contemporary worldwide scene is a pivotal endeavor, particularly directly following the Coronavirus pandemic. As the world wrestles with continuous difficulties and makes progress toward recuperation, understanding and relieving these dangers is fundamental for building strength and guaranteeing economical turn of events. This investigation dives into key areas of likely dangers and weaknesses, including wellbeing emergencies, monetary vulnerabil-ities, international strains, natural dangers, and innovative weaknesses.

1. **Wellbeing Emergencies and Pandemics:**
1. **Arising Irresistible Sicknesses:** The Coronavirus pandemic has featured the weakness of worldwide wellbeing frameworks to arising irresistible illnesses. The gamble of new infections and microbes crossing from creatures to people represents a continuous danger. Quick urbanization, deforestation, and expanded worldwide travel add to the potential for overflow occasions, requiring watchfulness in observing and overseeing zoonotic sicknesses.
2. **Antibody Aversion and Access:** In spite of headways in immunization advancement, immunization reluctance and inconsistent access present dangers to worldwide wellbeing. Variations in antibody appropriation, strategic difficulties, and reluctance powered by deception can prevent mass vaccination endeavors. These difficulties highlight the requirement for global coordinated effort, impartial immunization appropriation, and vigorous general wellbeing correspondence methodologies.
3. **Antimicrobial Opposition:** The raising danger of antimicrobial obstruction (AMR) represents an extreme gamble to worldwide wellbeing. Abuse of antimicrobials in medical care and horticulture adds to the advancement of medication safe kinds of microorganisms, making diseases harder to treat. Relieving AMR requires composed endeavors to control anti-infection use, put resources into new treatments, and improve worldwide reconnaissance to screen opposition designs.
4. **Wellbeing Disparities:** Constant wellbeing imbalances inside and between nations intensify weaknesses. Financial variables, lacking medical care foundation, and restricted admittance to fundamental administrations add to variations in wellbeing results. Tending to these weaknesses requires an exhaustive methodology, remembering ventures for essential medical care, social determinants of wellbeing, and endeavors to guarantee widespread wellbeing inclusion.

2. **Financial Vulnerabilities:**

1. **Worldwide Financial Abberations:** Monetary vulnerabilities and inconsistencies endure as nations recuperate from the effect of the pandemic. The lopsided appropriation of financial recuperation, with specific areas and locales bouncing back more rapidly than others, compounds worldwide monetary variations. Primary issues, for example, pay imbalance, insufficient social security nets, and restricted monetary strength among weak populaces present continuous dangers to financial dependability.
2. **Obligation Weight:** The huge expansion in open obligation across numerous countries during the pandemic raises worries about long haul financial maintainability. Nations that executed broad boost estimates presently face the test of overseeing elevated degrees of obligation. The potential for obligation

emergencies in non-industrial countries, combined with the gamble of expanded loan costs, represents a danger to monetary recuperation and monetary strength.

3. **Exchange Interruptions and Protectionism:** Progressing international strains and the apparition of protectionist exchange arrangements present dangers to worldwide stock chains and monetary relationship. Disturbances in global exchange can affect financial development, lead to inflated costs for organizations, and upset the progression of labor and products. Reinforcing worldwide participation and multilateral economic accords becomes fundamental in relieving these dangers.

4. **Work Uprooting and Disparity:** Sped up innovative headways, exacerbated by the pandemic, can possibly dislodge customary positions and develop pay imbalance. Robotization, man-made brainpower, and computerized change might prompt work market shifts, requiring proactive measures for reskilling and upskilling the labor force. Inability to address these difficulties could increase social disparities and prevent comprehensive financial development.

3. International Pressures:

1. **Rising International Competitions:** Raising international strains among significant powers present dangers to worldwide soundness. Exchange questions, vital rivalry, and philosophical conflicts can prompt expanded unpredictability in global relations. Expected flashpoints, like regional debates, digital fighting, and military showdowns, make vulnerabilities that can influence financial and political scenes worldwide.

2. **Philanthropic Emergencies and Mass Relocations:** International contentions, exacerbated by monetary and natural variables, can prompt compassionate emergencies and mass movements. Uprooted populaces face increased weaknesses, and the stress on have nations' assets can heighten strains.
Tending to the main drivers of struggles and encouraging conciliatory goals are essential to relieving the dangers related with international precariousness.

3. **Patriotism and Disintegration of Multilateralism:** The resurgence of patriotism and a retreat from multilateralism present dangers to worldwide joint effort. Disintegration of helpful systems, withdrawal from peaceful accords, and the debilitating of worldwide foundations can prevent aggregate reactions to shared difficulties. Supporting the significance of multilateral collaboration becomes principal in tending to worldwide dangers.

4. Ecological Dangers:

1. **Environmental Change Effects:** The heightening effects of environmental change, including outrageous climate occasions, rising ocean levels, and

disturbances to biological systems, present extreme dangers to the planet. The financial, social, and ecological outcomes of uncontrolled environmental change can prompt boundless dislodging, food frailty, and expanded recurrence of catastrophic events. Moderating environment gambles requires earnest worldwide endeavors to diminish ozone harming substance emanations and adjust to evolving conditions.

2. **Biodiversity Misfortune:** The deficiency of biodiversity presents dangers to environments, food security, and human prosperity. Living space annihilation, contamination, and environmental change add to the downfall of species variety. The potential outcomes incorporate interruptions to environments, diminished strength to infections, and the deficiency of important hereditary assets. Protection endeavors and maintainable practices are basic to address these weaknesses.

3. **Normal Asset Consumption:** Unreasonable utilization of regular assets, including water, timberlands, and minerals, presents dangers to environmental equilibrium and human jobs. Overexploitation, deforestation, and contamination add to asset consumption. Carrying out mindful asset the board works on, progressing to roundabout economies, and encouraging maintainable utilization designs are basic in moderating these dangers.

5. Mechanical Weaknesses:

1. **Network safety Dangers:** The rising dependence on computerized advances uncovered social orders and economies to online protection dangers. Cyberattacks on basic framework, information breaks, and ransomware assaults can have serious financial and cultural outcomes. Reinforcing network safety measures, global joint effort on computerized administration, and putting resources into versatile advanced framework are vital for address these weaknesses.

2. **Mechanical Joblessness:** The fast speed of innovative progressions, including mechanization and computerized reasoning, raises worries about mechanical joblessness. Work uprooting because of computerization can prompt social and financial disturbances, especially if sufficient measures for labor force reskilling and work market flexibility are not set up. Offsetting mechanical advancement with social contemplations is critical to alleviate these dangers.

3. **Advanced Imbalance:** The computerized partition, described by variations in admittance to computerized advances and the web, compounds cultural disparities. Absence of admittance to advanced assets blocks instructive open doors, limits monetary interest, and augments social holes. Connecting the advanced separation requires purposeful endeavors to guarantee general admittance to computerized foundation and innovation schooling.

8.3 Recommendations for building long-term economic resilience

Fabricating long haul financial versatility requires a multi-layered and key methodology that tends to weaknesses, cultivates flexibility, and advances feasible turn of events. The examples gained from the difficulties presented by the Coronavirus pandemic highlight the significance of proactive measures to fortify economies against future shocks. This investigation frames key proposals for building long haul monetary versatility, including financial strategies, medical care frameworks, social security nets, ecological maintainability, and mechanical development.

1. **Expansion of Monetary Designs:**

   Enhancing monetary designs is central to building flexibility against outside shocks. Overreliance on unambiguous areas, as seen during the pandemic, can prompt weaknesses. State run administrations and organizations ought to put resources into expansion procedures, advancing the development of different ventures. This includes supporting arising areas like innovation, sustainable power, and medical care. Broadening upgrades monetary solidness as well as makes a more versatile and responsive financial scene.

2. **Interest in Medical services Framework:**

   A powerful medical care framework is a foundation of monetary flexibility. The pandemic uncovered weaknesses in medical services frameworks around the world, featuring the requirement for supported ventures. States ought to focus on medical care foundation advancement, guaranteeing sufficient emergency clinic limit, clinical supplies, and medical care faculty. Putting resources into innovative work, particularly in the fields of irresistible illnesses and general wellbeing, gets ready countries to answer actually to future wellbeing emergencies.

3. **Financial Strategies for Solidness and Adaptability:**

   Executing financial arrangements that balance soundness and adaptability is significant for long haul monetary strength.

   Legislatures ought to keep up with monetary discipline during stable periods, building financial cradles for seasons of emergency. Notwithstanding, adaptability is similarly critical to take into account convenient reactions to monetary slumps. Countercyclical financial approaches, for example, designated boost measures during downturns, can uphold monetary recuperation and alleviate the effect of outer shocks.

4. **Fortifying Social Wellbeing Nets:**

   Social security nets assume a crucial part in safeguarding weak populaces during financial shocks. States ought to focus on the foundation and reinforcing of social wellbeing nets, including joblessness benefits, medical care, and help programs for those out of luck. This locations prompt financial difficulties as well as upgrades cultural strength by decreasing disparities and advancing comprehensive monetary development.

5. **Upgraded Worldwide Coordinated effort on Wellbeing:**

Worldwide coordinated effort on wellbeing drives is basic for handling pandemics and arising wellbeing dangers. Nations ought to build up global organizations, share best practices, and team up on innovative work. Drives like COVAX, pointed toward guaranteeing impartial admittance to immunizations, ought to be extended and supported. Reinforcing the World Wellbeing Association (WHO) and other global wellbeing offices is crucial for cultivating an organized worldwide reaction to wellbeing emergencies.

6. **Ecological Maintainability and Green Drives:**
Implanting natural manageability into financial arrangements is fundamental for long haul strength. Legislatures ought to focus on green drives, put resources into environmentally friendly power, and change toward roundabout economies. Feasible practices add to ecological preservation as well as upgrade financial proficiency and relieve gambles related with environmental change. The coordination of natural contemplations into monetary direction guarantees a stronger and reasonable future.

7. **Interest in Innovation and Digitalization:**
Mechanical advancement and computerized change are key drivers of monetary versatility. State run administrations and organizations ought to put resources into innovation foundation, advance computerized proficiency, and cultivate development environments. Embracing computerized reasoning, information examination, and arising innovations improves financial intensity and readiness. The digitalization of cycles, including internet business and remote work, works with congruity during emergencies as well as positions economies for supported development.

8. **Flexibility in Supply Chains:**
The pandemic featured weaknesses in worldwide stockpile chains, underlining the requirement for strength. Legislatures and organizations ought to reexamine and broaden supply chains, lessening reliance on unambiguous districts. This includes key accumulating of fundamental products, encouraging local coordinated efforts, and utilizing innovation for constant inventory network perceivability. Tough stockpile chains improve monetary security, even despite disturbances.

9. **Interest in Schooling and Labor force Improvement:**
Training and labor force improvement are basic parts of financial versatility. Legislatures ought to put resources into schooling systems that cultivate versatility, decisive reasoning, and computerized abilities. Also, reskilling and upskilling drives ought to be elevated to address advancing position market requests. An exceptionally talented and versatile labor force is fundamental for ventures to explore mechanical headways and financial changes.

10. **Improved Monetary Guideline and Hazard The executives:**
Reinforcing monetary guideline and chance administration structures is fundamental for forestalling and relieving financial emergencies. Legislatures ought

to execute and implement hearty administrative measures to guarantee the soundness of monetary establishments. This incorporates checking fundamental dangers, upgrading straightforwardness, and creating instruments for early intercession. Solid gamble the board rehearses add to monetary soundness and diminish the probability of fundamental disappointments.

11. **Local area and Territorial Versatility Arranging:**
Building monetary versatility ought to reach out to local area and territorial levels. Neighborhood states and organizations ought to take part in versatility arranging that records for local monetary qualities, weaknesses, and ecological variables. Local area level drives, for example, debacle readiness, supportable improvement undertakings, and neighborhood financial enhancement, add to generally flexibility by making versatile and interconnected frameworks.

12. **Discretion and Multilateralism:**

Worldwide strategy and multilateral collaboration are significant for tending to worldwide difficulties. States ought to take part in political endeavors to determine international pressures and reinforce global coordinated effort. Multilateral associations, like the Unified Countries, ought to be upheld and improved to upgrade their ability to on the whole resolve worldwide issues. Political discourse and adherence to worldwide standards add to a steady and cooperative global climate.

Chapter 9

Conclusion

All in all, exploring the post-pandemic period requires a far reaching and versatile methodology that tends to the multi-layered difficulties looked by the worldwide local area. The Coronavirus pandemic has been a turning point, highlighting the interconnectedness of our reality, uncovering weaknesses, and featuring the basic for coordinated effort and versatility. The excursion toward renewing flourishing and diagramming a course for economical improvement requests an aggregate obligation to gaining from the examples of the pandemic and carrying out groundbreaking systems.

The extraordinary difficulties presented by the pandemic, from wellbeing emergencies to monetary vulnerabilities, international pressures, natural dangers, and mechanical weaknesses, require a change in outlook in how social orders and countries approach flexibility. As we ponder the significant effect of the pandemic on worldwide economies and social orders, it becomes obvious that the way ahead requires a cautious difficult exercise — one that considers the prompt recuperation needs as well as the basic for long haul manageability.

The ID of possible dangers and weaknesses, as investigated in prior segments, gives a guide to proactive and key navigation. It highlights the significance of strengthening medical care frameworks, executing financial arrangements that balance solidness and adaptability, and putting resources into broadened and manageable monetary designs. Besides, perceiving the job of innovation in financial versatility, the requirement for strong stockpile chains, and the basic of addressing natural difficulties add to an all encompassing comprehension of the perplexing exchange of variables molding the post-pandemic scene.

Proposals for building long haul financial versatility, going from differentiating monetary designs to upgrading worldwide cooperation on wellbeing, from putting resources into innovation and digitalization to invigorating social security nets, highlight the interconnected idea of flexibility building techniques. These proposals give an outline to legislatures, organizations, and networks to make versatile, comprehensive, and maintainable monetary frameworks that can endure future shocks.

Essentially, the recovery of thriving post-pandemic is unpredictably connected to worldwide cooperation and discretionary endeavors. The meaning of discretion and multilateralism couldn't possibly be more significant in cultivating a climate of dependability and collaboration. Settling international pressures, reinforcing worldwide foundations, and sticking to shared standards are fundamental for establishing a helpful worldwide climate that advances financial development, harmony, and versatility.

Looking forward, the expected future patterns, including the speed increase of computerized change, an emphasis on supportability, and the reshaping of work models, offer open doors for development and development. Embracing these patterns while tending to industrious difficulties, for example, disparity, obligation weights, and environmental change, requires a ground breaking and versatile methodology. Maintainable advancement objectives should be at the very front of recuperation endeavors, guaranteeing that monetary development lines up with social prosperity and natural stewardship.

The post-pandemic recuperation isn't just about beating prompt difficulties yet in addition about impelling a key change in how social orders conceptualize and seek after thriving. The idea of working back better infers a pledge to making more even-handed, comprehensive, and economical economies. It includes a takeoff from old ideal models that might have added to weaknesses, and a promise to encouraging versatile frameworks equipped for enduring future shocks.

As countries wrestle with the intricacies of recuperation, the job of development and innovation arises as an impetus for positive change. Utilizing mechanical progressions for monetary development, work creation, and cultural prosperity is significant.

Adjusting the advantages of mechanical advancement with moral contemplations, resolving issues of computerized disparity, and guaranteeing mindful development are necessary to molding a future where innovation turns into a power for positive change.

The interweaved difficulties of reskilling the labor force, tending to joblessness, and decreasing disparity highlight the significance of human-driven ways to deal with monetary recuperation. Putting resources into instruction, supporting labor force advancement programs, and carrying out strategies that focus on inclusivity are essential for guaranteeing that the advantages of financial development are shared fairly. The flexibility of economies is, in numerous ways, dependent upon the versatility and flexibility of the labor force.

The accentuation on territorial viewpoints, perceiving the exceptional difficulties looked by changed areas and supporting for cross-provincial coordinated effort, features the need for nuanced and setting explicit methodologies. A one-size-fits-all approach is lacking in a world described by different monetary, social, and ecological scenes. Territorial collaboration can improve the viability of recuperation endeavors and add to the production of versatile and locally important arrangements.

The excursion toward maintainable turn of events and worldwide financial flexibility isn't without its investigates and likely inadequacies. Perceiving and addressing these difficulties is essential to refining and fortifying recuperation procedures. From the likely entanglements of strategy executions to the drawn out ramifications of particular measures, a basic evaluation of the picked way is important. This includes constant assessment, versatile policymaking, and a receptiveness to gaining from the two triumphs and disappointments.

The job of worldwide collaboration arises as a key part chasing worldwide financial strength. Cooperative endeavors among countries and worldwide organizations, investigated top to bottom, give an establishment to tending to shared difficulties. The accentuation on investigating worldwide drives for monetary recuperation and cultivating global fortitude supports the interconnectedness of the worldwide local area. It highlights that genuine versatility lies not in segregation but rather in that frame of mind of cooperative undertakings and shared obligation to shared objectives.

Developments in innovation and computerized change, investigated as urgent parts of recuperation, offer a brief look into the eventual fate of financial advancement. The effect of mechanical progressions on financial recuperation and the possibilities for supported development through advancement portray a dynamic and quickly advancing scene. Embracing these developments requires a proactive methodology that adjusts the advantages of innovation with moral contemplations and cultural prosperity.

The significance of integrating maintainability into monetary recuperation plans, investigated inside and out, is a demonstration of the developing acknowledgment of ecological objectives. The investigation of nations focusing on green drives and the sensitive harmony between monetary development and natural protection underline the requirement for a change in outlook. The reconciliation of maintainable practices into monetary strategies isn't just a reaction to ecological difficulties yet in addition an essential push toward long haul strength.

The basic of reskilling and labor force transformation is urgent in tending to the advancing position market post-pandemic. The examination of movements in the gig market and methodologies for reskilling the labor force stresses the requirement for readiness and nonstop learning. Tending to the difficulties of joblessness and disparity requires a comprehensive methodology that consolidates designated strategies, instructive drives, and coordinated effort among states and organizations.

The assessment of novel difficulties looked by changed areas and the near examination of local recuperation techniques feature the significance of setting explicit methodologies. Potential open doors for cross-territorial coordinated effort, investigated top to bottom, give roads to sharing information, assets, and best practices. Building flexibility at the territorial level adds to the general strength and versatility of the worldwide financial framework.

The investigation of future viewpoint and worldwide financial versatility brings the conversation round trip. Considering the headway made in the post-pandemic recuperation, the examination highlights the significance of versatility, worldwide collaboration, and practical turn of events. The future standpoint is portrayed by the proceeded with need for transformation, the basic of worldwide collaboration, and the quest for supportable and comprehensive development.

In outline, the excursion toward reviving success and exploring the worldwide monetary recuperation post-pandemic is a complicated and multi-layered try. It requires a cautious thought of wellbeing, financial, social, ecological, and innovative aspects. The examples gained from the difficulties presented by the pandemic proposition significant experiences and highlight the significance of strength, flexibility, and worldwide cooperation.

As social orders and countries push ahead, the accentuation ought to be on working back better — making monetary frameworks that are strong even with shocks as well as fair, comprehensive, and manageable. The way forward requires a promise to learning, development, and cooperation. By executing the proposals illustrated, tending to difficulties proactively, and cultivating a feeling of versatility, the worldwide local area can produce a future that is described by shared thriving, ecological stewardship, and a promise to the prosperity of all. The post-pandemic recuperation isn't simply a stage; it is a valuable chance to shape a stronger, comprehensive, and supportable world.

9.1 Summarization of key findings and insights

In summing up the broad investigation of rejuvenating thriving and exploring the worldwide monetary recuperation post-pandemic, key discoveries and experiences arise across different aspects, enveloping wellbeing, financial matters, international relations, ecological supportability, innovation, and social elements. The accompanying gives a dense outline of the remarkable focuses got from the top to bottom examination:

1. **Pandemic's Effect on Worldwide Economies:**
   The underlying examination dug into the significant effect of the pandemic on worldwide economies. The quick financial aftermath was described by disturbances to supply chains, decreases in shopper spending, and withdrawals in different areas. Legislatures overall carried out exceptional measures, including lockdowns and monetary upgrade bundles, to relieve the financial slump. Notwithstanding, the effect was lopsided, with specific areas and locales encountering more extreme results.

2. **Investigation of the Prompt Financial Aftermath:**
   Looking at the quick monetary aftermath during the pandemic uncovered the weakness of worldwide financial frameworks to outer shocks. Areas like travel, cordiality, and customary retail confronted significant downfalls, while innovation, medical services, and online business experienced development. The profundity of the monetary compression highlighted the interconnectedness of worldwide business sectors and the requirement for versatile systems to explore the vulnerabilities presented by such emergencies.

3. **Assessment of Areas Generally Impacted and Abberations in Effect:**
   An investigation of the areas most impacted by the pandemic featured

abberations in the effect on various ventures. Customary areas dependent on actual presence experienced more than those embracing computerized change. Moreover, the examination highlighted the financial incongruities, with weak populaces confronting unbalanced difficulties. The inconsistencies underlined the requirement for comprehensive recuperation methodologies to address fundamental imbalances.

4. **Illustrations Gained from the Emergency and the Requirement for Versatile Monetary Systems:**
The assessment of illustrations gained from the emergency accentuated the basic for versatile monetary techniques. Versatility arose as a focal subject, encouraging states, organizations, and people to be proactive in expecting and relieving future shocks. The significance of nimble policymaking, adaptable monetary designs, and a
obligation to persistent learning were highlighted as fundamental parts of post-pandemic recuperation.

5. **Strategy Reactions and Upgrade Measures:**
As states around the world answered the financial difficulties presented by the pandemic, an examination of strategy reactions and upgrade estimates uncovered the changed methodologies took on. Financial boost bundles, money related arrangement mediations, and social help programs were executed to settle economies and safeguard weak populaces. The progress of these actions relied upon variables like practicality, designated allotment of assets, and the capacity to adjust to advancing conditions.

6. **Appraisal of Government Intercessions and Financial Arrangements Around the world:**
An extensive evaluation of government intercessions and monetary strategies overall featured the significance of a planned and complex methodology. While improvement estimates assumed an essential part in deflecting a more profound monetary emergency, difficulties, for example, rising public obligation and potential inflationary tensions required cautious adjustment of strategy reactions. The examination stressed the requirement for legislatures to work out some kind of harmony between transient adjustment and long haul financial supportability.

7. **Effective Approach Executions:**
An investigation of fruitful strategy executions exhibited occasions where state run administrations successfully dealt with the monetary aftermath. Nations that executed deft and designated measures, upheld by solid organizations and powerful administration, showed versatility even with difficulties. Examples of overcoming adversity gave significant bits of knowledge into the elements adding to fruitful monetary recuperation and the significance of versatile policymaking.

8. **Study of Possible Deficiencies and Long haul Suggestions:**
Nonetheless, the examination didn't avoid studying expected inadequacies and

long haul ramifications of specific arrangement measures. Concerns with respect to inflationary tensions, inconsistent dissemination of improvement benefits, and the gamble of monetary insecurity were tended to. This basic assessment underscored the requirement for ceaseless checking, change of procedures, and a nuanced comprehension of the potential compromises related with strategy choices.

9. **The Job of Global Collaboration:**
   The investigation of the job of worldwide participation enlightened the meaning of cooperative endeavors among countries and worldwide establishments. The pandemic highlighted the interconnectedness of worldwide difficulties, requiring an aggregate reaction. Cooperative drives in immunization dissemination, environmental change relief, and monetary inclusivity exhibited the requirement for reinforced global collaboration systems and political exchange to really address shared difficulties.

10. **Investigation of Cooperative Endeavors Among Countries and Worldwide Establishments:**
    A top to bottom investigation of cooperative endeavors among countries and worldwide establishments gave experiences into the possibility to aggregate activity in tending to worldwide difficulties. Drives, for example, antibody sharing, environment agrees, and cooperative exploration exemplified the force of worldwide participation. The investigation underscored the significance of encouraging a feeling of coordinated effort, straightforwardness, and shared liability on the worldwide stage.

11. **Assessment of Worldwide Drives Focused on Monetary Recuperation:**
    An assessment of worldwide drives focused on monetary recuperation exhibited the variety of approaches took on by nations and global associations. From framework speculations to green recuperation plans, countries sought after different procedures to prod monetary development. The investigation highlighted the requirement for setting explicit and inventive arrangements, taking into account the extraordinary difficulties looked by changed districts.

12. **Difficulties and Open doors in Encouraging Worldwide Fortitude:**
    Difficulties and open doors in encouraging worldwide fortitude were investigated exhaustively. While the pandemic featured occasions of worldwide fortitude, difficulties like immunization patriotism, international pressures, and financial inconsistencies presented hindrances to a brought together reaction. The investigation highlighted the basic of conquering these difficulties through conciliatory endeavors, evenhanded asset conveyance, and a common obligation to the prosperity of humankind.

13. **Developments in Innovation and Computerized Change:**
    Advancements in innovation and computerized change arose as key drivers of financial recuperation and future development. The examination exhibited how mechanical headways, from telemedicine to remote work arrangements,

assumed a significant part in adjusting to the difficulties presented by the pandemic. The investigation accentuated the extraordinary capability of innovation in reshaping ventures, setting out new open doors, and upgrading in general monetary strength.

14. **Effect of Innovative Headways on Financial Recuperation:**
An assessment of the effect of mechanical headways on monetary recuperation highlighted the groundbreaking idea of advancement. The coordination of advanced innovations worked with business progression during the pandemic as well as sped up existing patterns like internet business, robotization, and information investigation. The examination featured the requirement for proactive systems to tackle the advantages of innovative progressions while tending to potential difficulties like work removal.

15. **Ventures Utilizing Advanced Change:**
Enterprises utilizing computerized change were investigated, displaying the way that different areas adjusted to the advanced time. From medical care to instruction, the investigation uncovered how ventures integrated innovation to improve proficiency, openness, and strength. The investigation stressed the significance of embracing computerized change as an essential basic for organizations and legislatures the same.

16. **Possibilities for Supported Development Through Mechanical Advancement:**
Possibilities for supported development through mechanical development portrayed a future where development keeps on driving financial advancement. The examination featured the potential for arising innovations, like computerized reasoning, biotechnology, and environmentally friendly power, to emphatically shape the monetary scene. The investigation highlighted the significance of cultivating a climate that empowers development and tackles the maximum capacity of mechanical headways.

17. **Manageable Turn of events and Green Drives:**
The basic of manageable turn of events and green drives was a common topic all through the investigation. The investigation underlined the significance of integrating maintainability into monetary recuperation plans. Nations focusing on green drives and the fragile harmony between monetary development and natural protection were investigated exhaustively. The examination highlighted the requirement for a change in perspective towards naturally cognizant strategies for long haul monetary strength.

18. **Significance of Integrating Maintainability into Monetary Recuperation Plans:**
The significance of integrating maintainability into financial recuperation plans was investigated top to bottom. The investigation highlighted that monetary development should line up with natural stewardship to guarantee long haul versatility. Techniques, for example, progressing to sustainable power, advancing

round economies, and coordinating natural contemplations into policymaking were featured as fundamental parts of a maintainable recuperation.

19. **Nations Focusing on Green Drives:**
An investigation of nations focusing on green drives exhibited worldwide endeavors to change towards economical practices. Instances of countries putting resources into sustainable power, executing eco-accommodating strategies, and setting aggressive environment targets featured the developing acknowledgment of the connection between natural manageability and monetary strength. The examination underscored the requirement for an aggregate obligation to practical improvement objectives.

20. **Offsetting Financial Development with Natural Protection:**
Offsetting monetary development with natural preservation arose as a focal test and opportunity. The investigation dove into the sensitive balance expected to accomplish maintainable turn of events. The examination highlighted the significance of systems that invigorate financial development as well as focus on preservation, biodiversity, and capable asset the executives.

21. **Reskilling and Labor force Transformation:**
The basic of reskilling and labor force transformation was a basic concentration, tending to the changes in the gig market post-pandemic. The examination inspected how sped up mechanical progressions and advancing position requests require proactive measures for reskilling and upskilling the labor force. The investigation accentuated the job of schooling, preparing programs, and cooperative endeavors among legislatures and enterprises in setting up the labor force for what's to come.

22. **Examination of Movements in the Gig Market Post-Pandemic:**
An exhaustive examination of movements in the gig market post-pandemic gave bits of knowledge into the developing idea of work. The investigation featured the effect of robotization, remote work patterns, and the rise of new position jobs. The investigation highlighted the requirement for spry labor force methodologies that line up with mechanical progressions and changing industry requests.

23. **Methodologies for Reskilling the Labor force to Satisfy Developing Needs:**
Systems for reskilling the labor force to fulfill advancing needs were investigated exhaustively. The investigation stressed the significance of designated reskilling programs, coordinated effort between instructive foundations and businesses, and government drives to work with a smooth progress for laborers into arising areas. The investigation featured the job of constant learning in guaranteeing labor force flexibility.

24. **Tending to the Difficulties of Joblessness and Disparity:**
Tending to the difficulties of joblessness and disparity arose as a basic cultural goal. The examination dug into the diverse idea of these difficulties, perceiving the requirement for thorough strategies that advance work creation, social

wellbeing nets, and comprehensive monetary development. The investigation underlined that tending to these difficulties requires a comprehensive methodology including government mediations, confidential area drives, and local area level systems.

25. **Provincial Viewpoints on Recuperation:**
Inspecting territorial viewpoints on recuperation uncovered the special difficulties looked by changed districts.
From abberations in medical care framework to differing financial designs, the examination featured the requirement for setting explicit recuperation methodologies. The investigation underscored that recuperation plans should think about provincial subtleties and connect with nearby networks to construct versatile and strong frameworks.

26. **Assessment of One of a kind Difficulties Looked by Changed Locales:**
The assessment of interesting difficulties looked by changed areas gave bits of knowledge into the variety of financial scenes. The examination highlighted that variables like geological area, existing monetary designs, and social elements add to differed difficulties. The investigation featured the significance of fitting recuperation systems to address district explicit requirements and encouraging territorial coordinated effort.

27. **Near Examination of Territorial Recuperation Methodologies:**
A near examination of local recuperation methodologies displayed the assorted methodologies took on by countries in various regions of the planet. The investigation uncovered that fruitful recuperation systems think about provincial qualities, weaknesses, and financial settings. The investigation stressed the significance of sharing prescribed procedures and illustrations figured out how to work with cross-territorial learning and cooperation.

28. **Open doors for Cross-Provincial Cooperation:**
Investigating open doors for cross-provincial cooperation featured the potential for shared learning and asset dividing between countries. The examination highlighted the advantages of cooperative drives that rise above geological limits. The investigation stressed that cultivating cross-territorial cooperation adds to building a more interconnected and strong worldwide financial framework.

29. **Future Standpoint and Worldwide Financial Strength:**
The investigation of future standpoint and worldwide financial strength gave a forward-looking viewpoint. Thinking about the headway made in the post-pandemic recuperation, the examination featured the continuous requirement for versatility, worldwide participation, and supportable turn of events. The future viewpoint underscored the continuation of patterns like computerized change, supportability drives, and the reshaping of work models.

30. **Reflection on the Headway Made in the Post-Pandemic Recuperation:**
A reflection on the headway made in the post-pandemic recuperation highlighted the strength of countries and social orders in exploring remarkable

difficulties. The examination perceived the achievements in immunization dissemination, monetary bounce back, and cooperative drives. The investigation underscored the significance of expanding on these triumphs while addressing steady difficulties to guarantee a strong and supported recuperation.

31. **Recognizable proof of Possible Dangers and Weaknesses:**

Recognizing likely dangers and weaknesses in the post-pandemic world shaped an essential part of the examination. The investigation recognized that vulnerabilities, going from wellbeing emergencies to monetary, ecological, and innovative dangers, keep on molding the worldwide scene. The investigation accentuated the significance of proactive gamble the executives, worldwide participation, and versatile procedures to address these difficulties.

9.2 Call to action for sustained global cooperation

The broad investigation of reviving flourishing and exploring the worldwide monetary recuperation post-pandemic joins on a convincing source of inspiration for supported worldwide collaboration. The intricacies and interdependencies uncovered by the Coronavirus pandemic interest a brought together and cooperative reaction from countries, foundations, and people the same. This source of inspiration stretches out past quick recuperation endeavors to imagine a future where worldwide collaboration turns into the bedrock for building versatile, comprehensive, and reasonable economies.

The principal basic in this source of inspiration is the support of worldwide cooperation in medical care. The pandemic distinctly outlined the requirement for an aggregate and facilitated reaction to wellbeing emergencies. Admittance to immunizations, clinical supplies, and best practices should be generally shared. Reinforcing worldwide wellbeing frameworks, supporting innovative work limits, and laying out a structure for quick reaction to arising dangers are basic parts. Multilateral establishments, drove by a vigorous World Wellbeing Association, ought to assume a focal part in working with such coordinated effort, guaranteeing that no country is abandoned chasing general wellbeing.

Similarly vital is the obligation to comprehensive monetary recuperation. Worldwide collaboration should focus on systems that address the lopsided effect of the pandemic on weak populaces. Social security nets, schooling drives, and designated financial help projects ought to be intended to lift the most underestimated networks. A comprehensive recuperation isn't just an ethical objective yet in addition a monetary one, as versatile social orders are based on the groundwork of shared flourishing. Worldwide associations, as a team with public states and NGOs, ought to support drives that span financial holes and advance correspondence.

The source of inspiration stretches out to the domain of natural manageability. The dire need to battle environmental change and safeguard biodiversity requires brought together worldwide endeavors. Countries should focus on aggressive carbon decrease targets, put resources into environmentally friendly power, and change to round economies.

Cooperative drives, for example, worldwide environment concurs, ought to be strengthened to guarantee that natural stewardship is at the very front of recuperation plans. The common obligation regarding the planet's prosperity ought to rise above international limits, cultivating an aggregate obligation to defending the climate for people in the future.

Mechanical development, a foundation of financial recuperation, requests a cooperative methodology. Countries ought to pool assets for innovative work, share mechanical expertise, and lay out global guidelines for arising advances. The advanced gap, featured during the pandemic, ought to be addressed through drives that guarantee general admittance to computerized framework and innovation schooling. A guarantee to dependable and moral innovative improvement ought to direct global joint efforts, relieving potential dangers related with headways like man-made consciousness and robotization.

A basic part of supported worldwide collaboration is the cultivating of conciliatory answers for international pressures. The pandemic uncovered the delicacy of worldwide stockpile chains and the interconnectedness of economies. Strategy and discourse ought to be focused on over ill-disposed approaches, advancing an international climate helpful for financial steadiness. Worldwide foundations, including the Unified Countries, ought to act as stages for conciliatory commitment, compromise, and the foundation of standards that work with serene collaboration among countries.

In the domain of labor force transformation, a source of inspiration includes shared liability in tending to joblessness and reskilling challenges. Cooperative drives between state run administrations, organizations, and instructive establishments ought to be focused on to work with the change of the labor force into arising ventures. Worldwide organizations can give bits of knowledge into fruitful labor force improvement models, cultivating a worldwide biological system that upholds people in securing the abilities required for the positions representing things to come.

Local coordinated efforts should be empowered as a feature of the source of inspiration. Sharing accepted procedures, assets, and examples learned can improve the strength of areas confronting comparable difficulties. Stages for cross-local participation ought to be laid out, empowering countries to address exceptional provincial weaknesses all things considered. By cultivating a feeling of fortitude and common help, countries can explore shared difficulties all the more successfully, adding to the worldwide financial recuperation.

This source of inspiration likewise includes a guarantee to monetary strength and mindful financial strategies. Countries ought to team up on methodologies for overseeing public obligation, alleviating dangers to monetary frameworks, and guaranteeing that financial strategies line up with long haul monetary manageability.

Worldwide monetary organizations assume a vital part in working with exchange and collaboration on macroeconomic strategies, guaranteeing that the worldwide financial scene stays steady and strong.

Chasing reasonable turn of events, worldwide participation ought to stretch out to the prioritization of green drives. Countries should on the whole put resources into environmentally friendly power, preservation endeavors, and manageable practices. Peaceful accords, like the Paris Arrangement, ought to be reinforced, and instruments for sharing green advancements and aptitude ought to be laid out. The progress to a green economy requires a bound together obligation to making an amicable harmony between monetary development and natural safeguarding.

To support this source of inspiration, the job of global associations becomes fundamental. Foundations like the Unified Countries, the Global Money related Asset, and the World Bank ought to be sustained to act as channels for worldwide collaboration. Changes ought to improve their abilities to address contemporary difficulties, work with political exchanges, and direction global reactions to emergencies. Reinforcing the adequacy of these organizations guarantees that the worldwide local area has vigorous components for aggregate activity.

Instruction and information sharing structure a principal part of the source of inspiration. Countries ought to team up on drives that elevate admittance to quality training, trade scholarly ability, and work with social getting it. By encouraging a worldwide local area of educated and instructed people, countries can fabricate extensions of participation and common regard, rising above philosophical and social contrasts.

9.3 Hopeful outlook for a more resilient and equitable global economy post-pandemic

As we explore the intricate territory of renewing thriving and directing the worldwide monetary recuperation post-pandemic, a confident viewpoint arises, imagining a future set apart by flexibility, value, and shared flourishing. The illustrations gained from the difficulties of the Coronavirus pandemic give an establishment to groundbreaking change, cultivating an aggregate obligation to building a more comprehensive and economical worldwide economy.

At the core of this confident viewpoint is the acknowledgment that emergencies catalyze development and variation. The phenomenal difficulties presented by the pandemic have prodded sped up progressions in innovation, especially in the domains of medical care, remote work, and computerized change.

This mechanical jump offers the possibility of expanded proficiency, availability, and new open doors for monetary development. Embracing these developments can prepare for a more unique and versatile worldwide economy, cultivating areas that influence the force of information, man-made brainpower, and network.

In addition, the pandemic has brought to the very front the basic of putting resources into general wellbeing foundation and worldwide collaboration. The exceptional speed of immunization advancement and circulation, worked with by worldwide joint effort and logical development, exhibits the potential for aggregate activity in tending to worldwide difficulties. The confident standpoint imagines a reality where the examples gained from the pandemic brief supported interest in medical care frameworks, research, and worldwide collaboration to all the more likely plan for future wellbeing emergencies.

In the financial domain, the confident standpoint focuses on the potential for a more comprehensive recuperation. The weaknesses uncovered by the pandemic highlight the significance of tending to foundational imbalances. States, organizations, and global associations can jump all over this opportunity to execute strategies and drives that focus on friendly value. This incorporates designated help for weak populaces, interests in schooling and abilities improvement, and the making of financial designs that advance fair and comprehensive development.

The call for maintainability is a vital mainstay of the confident standpoint, stressing the earnestness of incorporating natural contemplations into monetary recuperation plans. Countries overall are progressively perceiving the natural connection between a solid climate and financial versatility. The reception of green drives, environmentally friendly power projects, and supportable strategic approaches can establish the groundwork for an ecologically cognizant worldwide economy. This obligation to maintainability not just addresses the squeezing danger of environmental change yet in addition cultivates the advancement of enterprises that line up with natural stewardship.

Mechanical headways, combined with a promise to maintainability, prepare for a green unrest in different areas. The confident standpoint imagines the far and wide reception of clean innovations, roundabout economies, and harmless to the ecosystem rehearses. This shift not just mitigates the ecological effect of monetary exercises yet additionally makes new roads for development and occupation creation. The quest for maintainability turns into a main thrust for financial development, adjusting monetary flourishing to ecological obligation.

A vital part of the confident standpoint is the accentuation on flexibility in supply chains and financial frameworks. The disturbances experienced during the pandemic highlight the requirement for enhanced and strong stockpile chains that can endure shocks.

The confident vision sees countries and organizations putting resources into techniques that improve inventory network strength, including territorial joint efforts, digitalization, and chance relief measures. This flexibility guarantees that the worldwide economy is more ready to explore unanticipated difficulties, adding to long haul strength.

Schooling arises as a foundation of the confident viewpoint, perceiving its urgent job in molding a versatile and versatile labor force. The speed increase of computerized change requires an emphasis on outfitting people with the abilities required for the positions representing things to come. The confident vision empowers interests in schooling systems that cultivate decisive reasoning, imagination, and advanced education. By enabling people with the instruments to explore a quickly evolving scene, countries can guarantee that their populaces are strategically situated to add to and benefit from the developing worldwide economy.

The confident viewpoint stretches out to the domain of worldwide participation, underscoring the discretionary and cooperative endeavors expected to address shared difficulties. International pressures, exchange questions, and patriot inclinations saw during the pandemic highlight the significance of encouraging a feeling of worldwide participation. The confident vision sees countries rising above contrasts, taking part in discretionary exchange, and working cooperatively through worldwide establishments to address prompt emergencies as well as long haul worldwide difficulties.

Moreover, the confident standpoint imagines a future where examples gained from the pandemic lead to a reconsideration of cultural qualities. The acknowledgment of the interconnectedness of worldwide prosperity prompts a shift toward values that focus on aggregate wellbeing, civil rights, and ecological maintainability. This social change cultivates a feeling of shared liability regarding the benefit of all, laying the foundation for a more caring and compassionate worldwide local area.

In the monetary area, the confident vision empowers the execution of capable financial strategies and global collaboration to guarantee long haul financial soundness. Countries can work together on methodologies for overseeing public obligation, staying away from monetary emergencies, and advancing practical financial development. Fortifying the strength of monetary frameworks through worldwide collaboration shields against the dangers of financial slumps and encourages a stable worldwide financial climate.

Territorial joint efforts assume a fundamental part in the confident viewpoint, perceiving the extraordinary difficulties and valuable open doors looked by changed districts. By encouraging cross-provincial drives, countries can share information, assets, and best works on, improving the versatility of every locale. This cooperative methodology recognizes that provincial qualities can add to the general security of the worldwide economy, making an organization of interconnected and commonly strong financial frameworks.

The confident viewpoint, in this manner, imagines a change in outlook — a takeoff from the same old thing toward a more reasonable, fair, and versatile worldwide economy. It relies on the aggregate responsibility of countries, organizations, and people to gain from the difficulties of the pandemic and execute groundbreaking techniques. By embracing development, focusing on maintainability, cultivating inclusivity, and fortifying worldwide participation, the confident vision expects a future where the worldwide economy rises out of the shadows of the pandemic with freshly discovered flexibility and a promise to shared success.

www.ingramcontent.com/pod-product-compliance
Lightning Source LLC
LaVergne TN
LVHW021711210726
843510LV00015B/1247